A
CLEAR
MIND

A

CLEAR

MIND

The Less Is More Mindset To Wellbeing And Performance

CHRIS FINN

ISBN-13: 9798287694586

Edited by Sean Bennett, Defining Chapter

To Alex and Louisa.
You both continually show me
how wonderful life can be.
You are such a joy to be around,
and I love you.

CONTENTS

FOREWORD

I was sitting having lunch at a personal development event when I met Chris for the first time. He sat opposite me and we got talking. He asked what I did for work, and when I said "I'm a coach," he said, "No way, me too." I could see the excitement in his eyes as he talked about what he does. He told me that he'd been a psychotherapist and senior lecturer in psychology, and then moved into coaching after he experienced the power it had to help people transform instantly, including himself. The more we talked, the more I saw that Chris had a very clear grounding in how we operate as human beings, he lit up with possibility. I was surprised at the depth of his understanding for human potential, but what really struck me was his ability to articulate every point in a way that was easy for me to absorb and understand.

Chris told me he was excited to help people, but wasn't sure where he would find clients as a coach, having come from a therapy background. We instantly hit it off and stayed in touch and Chris became a close friend. We regularly challenged each other and called each other up to a higher standard and still do to this day. What became apparent about Chris, which is rare in the personal development world, is that he has a superpower for turning insights into action. When he learns something new he applies it before most people have even finished hearing it. When he asked again about what he'd need to do to build a successful coaching practice, I smiled and said to him, "You'll have no problems helping people if you keep taking action like you do." Within just a few months, Chris had a full coaching practice and was sharing his wisdom with clients from all around the world. I wasn't one bit surprised.

We all see the world in different ways, that's the gift of our perspective, but this book shows you how the way you see the world is shaped, and how you can use this knowledge to create the life you want. The beautiful thing about what you'll experience in the upcoming pages is you won't be told what to do, or even what to think, but, if you stay open, instead you'll be given the opportunity to discover how to connect with your own wisdom. This book will help you unlock your true, authentic self and see the world from a deeper truth, your own wise lens. It will empower you.

The insights you gain from this book will connect you with an understanding in yourself that will allow you to know what you want, get unstuck anytime you need to and see yourself and the world with clarity. As someone who takes an inspiring amount of action, Chris will show you that you don't need to be given tools and action steps to change; instead, when your inner world changes, the steps will present themselves and you'll be ready to take them.

The blocks that we have aren't real, but they feel real. This book will help you remove your imaginary blocks by seeing the illusion of limitation clearly, so you can step into a world of pure possibility.

A clear mind is your journey to a life without limits, a life where you can see the world with clarity. I encourage you to let go of what you think you know and allow the insights in this book to remove any limits you thought you had, with the help of Chris's vast experience in psychology, the inside-out understanding, and human potential.

The good news is, Chris won't be giving you more stuff to learn or more things to do; in contrast, he will help you remove what's in the way so you can live the life you were meant to live.

Jon Prince,
The Perception Coach
Author of Start Before You're Ready

INTRODUCTION

We live in a time where stress, depression, anxiety, and burnout are commonplace. For many people, living an unfulfilled life has become the normal. Despite the advances we're making in technology and healthcare, prescription antidepressants are at an all-time high; people are living longer, but not happier lives.

With things like burnout and stress having become so normal, it can be almost suspicious to others if you're not struggling through life. One in five adults in the UK are currently on some form of antidepressant medication. What does that say about the state of modern life, and why is it made normal to be unhappy and unfulfilled?

NATURAL OR NORMAL?

Normal isn't the same as natural. Although it's common to struggle with life, we don't need to. We can be free. The answer lies in seeing through the thinking that is getting in our way.

What follows here is a guidebook to getting in touch with what's natural, and waking up from the thoughts that are clouding over your wellbeing and performance. My belief is that if you read this book with an open mind, it will leave you free to be whoever you want to be.

It can be surprising how much of what you want in life is, in fact, natural and innate. Here are some things that are natural and already available to you:

- Our wellbeing is innate and natural. We don't need to add anything to experience full and lasting peace and wellbeing. It's already there within you, beneath all your habitual thinking that says otherwise.
- We each have our own wisdom. You don't need to look elsewhere to navigate life, perform at your best, and create amazing things for yourself.
- We all have desires and passions, we just tend to bury them with our habitual thinking.
- We are all born inherently free. And that freedom is here now.
- Flow state is natural. Everyone has had the feeling of pure peace and presence, where you feel like you're exactly in the right place at the right time.

If all this is natural, what's then getting in the way of us being in this state all the time?

LIMITING BELIEFS

I've found that the reason we struggle and get stuck in life is because we have limiting thinking, and we believe things that aren't true, (like a superstition).

If you've ever felt that there's more to life, then you'll know it can feel like you're limited in some way, like you're living in a mind-made prison, a mental cage made of thought.

These mind-made prisons get in the way of us living the life we want to live. It's almost impossible to comprehend how much thought impacts and shapes our lives until you truly wake up to what's thought, and what's not.

If you keep coming across the same problems and patterns in your life, it's because you have some thinking that you can't see. We might call it a blind spot.

The beliefs we have can be operating in the background of our awareness all the time, shaping not only how we feel and act in life, but also filtering how we see and experience life itself.

It is these beliefs that create the struggles, stress, anxiety and low mood, and when you see through the thinking, you have a clear mind and are free.

In this book, you'll discover how much you create your own life experience with the power of thought, and my invitation to you is to see through those thought clouds. It's an invitation to see just how amazing you are, and how wonderful life can be when you don't let your limited habitual thinking get in the way.

When you shift your thinking, you'll find that what looked like a problem one moment isn't even there in the next. Because the most amazing thing with this transformative work is that…

Your entire experience of life can change in a single moment.

LIFE-CHANGING INSIGHTS

What follows in this book are the key insights from psychology that I believe make the most difference in people's lives.

This approach doesn't take years of therapy or learning any new techniques. It simply takes insight.

An insight is when you gain a deep understanding of how something works. I think the reason that insights about how life and psychology work are so important, is that when we know how something works, we are clear-minded and we work better.

When you get an insight for yourself, it's yours forever. Just like when you're learning to ride a bike and you get a sense of what balance feels like for the first time. You never fully forget, even if you've had a long break from riding, you now know the feel of balance. Once you've got these insights, it's obvious to you what to do in the moment with struggles and obstacles in life.

If at any point reading this book, things start to seem more complicated than they already are, this means something's not been communicated as I intended. If that does happen, I encourage you to let your thinking go and come back to the same part a little later, or skip it entirely. Remember the intention of this book is to clear your mind, not clutter it.

This book serves as a wake-up call to guide you, as simply

as possible, to the place where you'll rediscover your own inherent and innate freedom.

I've tried to keep it so that none of what I'm pointing to here is my opinion; it is simply grounded in psychology, and is just how things work.

This book contains the insights and perspectives that have made the most difference in my life and the lives of thousands of individuals I've worked with.

When you understand this simple approach, you'll likely find the following:

- You'll lose a taste for things that no longer work for you.
- You'll easily drop patterns that no longer serve you.
- Stress and anxiety will make less and less sense to you. You'll then find that you have the ability to drop both quicker, as you will see their true root cause.
- You'll find that you are more at peace and comfortable in your own skin.
- You will be more creative because you're in a less reactive state.
- You will be less attached to outcomes and more in love with the present moment.
- You will be more motivated to pursue things that you value and are important to you.
- You will find more love, joy, connection and fulfilment.

This work has a transformative quality and can happen to anyone at any moment.

TOOLS AND TECHNIQUES V TRANSFORMATION

When I worked as a lecturer in Cognitive Behavioural Therapy (CBT), I used to teach my students various strategies to help people cope with their experiences in life. What led me to leave my career in traditional psychology was that sometimes these multiple tools and techniques worked, but a lot of the time they didn't.

I wanted to understand more about the truth of what creates our experience of life and the root cause of human struggles. I wanted to understand the keys to wellbeing and performance.

My hope is that by reading this book and understanding more about how our psychology and life work, you will no longer be seeking tools and techniques to cope with life, because you'll be in your natural state of happiness. You don't need to add strategies when you can see the root cause of your struggles was some thinking that you didn't even know was there.

My approach is a *subtractive* thinking approach. Instead of adding to the overload of information already swimming around in your mind, I'll show you how to take things back to a clear mind and basic common sense that is already and always available within you.

In short, what I've come to see from leaving my successful career in traditional psychology is this:

People don't need more tools and techniques. They need less thinking clouding over their own true and brilliant nature.

UNDERSTANDING HOW THINGS WORK

Last summer, I went away on an extended family holiday with my Dad and siblings. One evening, we sat down together to play a new board game. My Dad poured us a glass of wine while one of my brothers read out the game's instructions.

We had a practice to get the hang of it, and after a while, we started getting immersed in the game. It soon became apparent that my Dad was consistently losing each round. Once I realised this, I asked, "Dad, what's going on with you? You keep losing".

"I don't understand the rules!" My Dad replied. "I wasn't paying attention when Mitch read the instructions out".

We took another look at the instructions, and once he understood how the game worked, he started playing much better, and he started winning some rounds.

Life is like a game. When you understand how the game works, you tend to play better. Think of this book as an instruction manual. Not one that tells you what to do or how to think and feel, but one that tells you how our psychology works so that you can get the best out of life and yourself. If life is a game to be lived, I want to understand how it works to get the most out of it.

Just like you might take a toy apart to understand how it works, understanding how we work psychologically is essential to our wellbeing and performance. If you don't understand how something works, how would you get the best out of it?

The more you align your understanding and actions with how life and your psychology really work, the smoother your life will be.

I've followed my passion for human potential and resilience now for two decades. In retrospect, it feels like I've been going through life picking up pieces of a jigsaw, which make up the truth of how our psychological experience really works. This book contains those jigsaw pieces in the form of life-changing insights, ones that I believe will help you create a life you love and rediscover the inner peace and wellbeing you were born with.

HOW TO USE THIS BOOK

Throughout this book, you'll find yourself looking inside frequently to check in with your own inner knowing. That's good. Everything you read will make perfect sense and feel simple, yet helpful. When most of my clients get an insight or breakthrough in a coaching session, it's usually just a moment of "oh yeah... of course!".

There are no tools, techniques or strategies in this book. This is not a how-to guide. This is a book purely based on life-changing insights that point to freedom. When reading what I have to say, you'll find yourself making more sense of your life and the struggles you've been experiencing. In that sense, you'll also wake up from the root cause of those problems.

I recommend that when you read this book, you read it all the way through, and then you go back and read it again. Due to its progressive nature, I think this is the way you'll get the most from it. Although chapter one needs to be the first chapter, you'll get more from it when you read it for the second time after you've read the rest of the book. As master coach Steve Chandler used to say 'Read once for information, read twice for transformation'.

Throughout the chapters are some reflection boxes where you can write down your own insights and thoughts. I encourage you to write in these boxes as you would a journal and make this book your own.

At the end of each chapter, you will also find some prompts for applying the insights in your own life. Use them. Only then will you gain the full benefit from this book.

When conversations appear in the book, names and details have been altered to protect confidentiality.

BUT HOW?

One of the questions you'll ask yourself throughout this book is, "How do I do that?"

"How do I let go of thought?"

"How do I raise my wellbeing or level of presence?"

"How, how, how?"

Because I'm pointing to what's natural, I will suggest that you already know how.

You know how to do all of these things on some level inside you. Just like you know how to breathe without thinking.

If you're still asking "how?", it means that you haven't really gotten the insight and you need to see it more deeply. When you get an understanding, you live it. You come from that place of getting it.

What you'll come to understand from reading this book is how much thought impacts your life. My hope is that by the end of this book, you won't be asking 'how?' because you'll see the truth, which is that;

You don't need to think your way out of a thought-created problem, you simply need to see through it.

CHAPTER 1

WAKING UP TO HOW YOUR MIND WORKS

'Reality is merely an illusion, albeit a very persistent one.'
Albert Einstein

What if your experience of life doesn't work the way it appears to?

One of my first real insights into how life works was in a psychology lecture on the mechanism of perception.

Up until this point, I had assumed we passively witness a fixed reality. That our eyes work like a camera, our ears like a microphone. I figured we take in an objective outside world via the senses, and that we interact with it in an unbiased way. What I studied showed me it doesn't work like that at all.

The lecture taught me something called top-down and

bottom-up processing, and how much of our experience comes purely from our senses, versus how much is created in the mental activity of our psychology.

What really happens is that information, such as wavelengths or sound waves, enters our senses. Then our senses relay electrical signals to our brain via sensory pathways. Once the brain receives these signals, it creates an internal psychological experience based on what it predicts must be outside, in the material world. This means our conscious perception is our own internal experience, and not an outside reality.

As an example of this, although it might be difficult to believe, we know that colours don't exist in nature. We experience the illusion of colour when certain cells in our eyes detect certain wavelengths of light, and then our brain interprets electrical signals, giving us the perceptual illusion of "green" or "orange", etc.

When it comes to perceptual phenomena, the condition I find most fascinating is something called Synaesthesia. A person with synaesthesia can experience smells when they look at colours, or hear music when they taste food. Their experience of life is vastly different to most people's, and this is because we have different kinds of mental activity hidden from our awareness, in the background, shaping our experience of life.

I was pondering what this all means, on the bus on the way home from university, when I noticed a van drive past with the word 'Shoplifting' written on the side. This snapped me out of my contemplation and into a new one. Why would a van be driving along advertising the fact that they were shoplifters? I took a second glance and was amazed to see that what was actually written were the words 'Shop Fitters'.

My brain had misread it. It had taken information from my senses and manipulated it without my awareness. I couldn't believe it could do this. It was like I couldn't trust my own eyes. Like my mind was creating my experience of life without me, on some level even knowing I was involved.

But what I experienced wasn't a feeling of distrust or fear. Instead, I felt a profound sense of excitement and possibility, along with a deep and lasting peace. I couldn't quite understand why I felt such freedom and peace, but it was as if I had woken from a dream. I dropped into a clear mind, and with that came a boost in wellbeing.

When we wake up to where our experience is coming from, life gets a whole lot easier and more enjoyable. We experience a greater sense of possibility and productivity.

PRE-CONSCIOUS PERCEPTION

Although it appears that we're perceiving an objective outside world (and it's usually quite practical that it works that way), what we're actually perceiving is our **interpretation** of an outside world.

Cognitive interpretation (or thought) has already occurred before you become aware of an object, which means that by the time you're aware of that object, you've already made sense of it in your own mind.

13

In other words, raw information from the outside world gets collapsed with our mental processes, so that by the time we're conscious of something, thought has already occurred, and we can't see the bare object or circumstance itself.

If what you're conscious of is your own mental activity, then that means that what you're experiencing is coming from inside you, not outside you, as it appears.

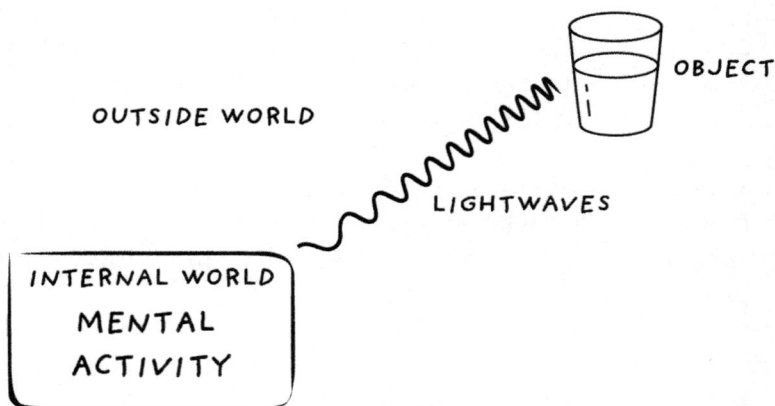

OUTSIDE WORLD

OBJECT

LIGHTWAVES

INTERNAL WORLD
MENTAL
ACTIVITY

WE'RE NOT CONSCIOUS OF THE
OBJECT, OR THE LIGHTWAVES.
WE'RE CONSCIOUS OF OUR OWN
MENTAL ACTIVITY.

What we're conscious of is a limited and subjective perceptual assumption based on how our brain is wired and how it's been conditioned by past experiences. Essentially, what I came to see is that our experience of life is psychological.

When I talk about this with my clients, I like to distinguish between situations and experience. A situation is objective and is there regardless of whether we think about it or not, and is independent of our experience.

Experience is our own, uniquely personal and subjective internal thoughts and feelings. Our own personal experience is independent of external circumstance, and whilst understandable, it is based on our own psychology and not the outside world.

Said another way:

We unconsciously both create and perceive our own experience of life, and we can become conscious of this process.

PSYCHOLOGY IS EVERYWHERE

There is not one single area of life that this doesn't impact. We live in a psychological reality where we are conscious of our perceptions. It doesn't look like this, but that's the illusion. Perhaps this is why we enjoy visual illusions so much, as they point to how our psychological system really works.

Like the dot-to-dot image that follows, the mind automatically creates the illusion of solidity. You see an owl, but the owl isn't inherent in the dots; it is created by your perception.

Inherent: Existing in something as a permanent, essential, or characteristic attribute. (Oxford English Dictionary)

In the same way that the owl looks real, our perception feels like an unequivocal reality. Our experience of life, which includes the contents of thoughts, emotions and sensory perceptions, is self-created, which means life, for us, is experienced from the inside-out, not the outside-in. Our experiences are, in turn, influenced by our various beliefs, which means we're limited to particular ways of experiencing life where we can't be aware of every possibility.

This is not to say that there is no such thing as an outside world, just that each individual person has his/her own individual perception of life and, whilst we experience meaning and the outside world as one and the same, if we look closely enough, we can begin to see that they're indeed separate in nature.

Like the owl, it looks like we're thinking about a fixed thing, but the truth is that between you and the thing that you're thinking about is a layer of thought.

You're only able to be aware of something because of the power of thought, which means that by the time you are aware of it, you've already had thinking. We can have thinking, and not even know that we have thinking. And in fact, this is often the case. We can have a lot of thinking about certain things like emotions, money, relationships, and life, and not even know it!

It's actually when we have less thinking about something that we tend to function better. When you see past the thinking that's getting in your way, you feel good, and you function well.

INSIDE-OUT

Perhaps it doesn't look or feel like we create life from the 'inside-out' most of the time. This is why there are a lot of misconceptions. Due to the tricks of the mind, it can sometimes appear that our inner experience is 100% due to our circumstances, and that our feelings are because of life, other people, and situations. But it doesn't work like that. This is really good news, as it means that we are not at the mercy of what happens to us.

Because our inner experience is created by us, it can and will change as soon as we change our level of consciousness, or our thinking. In other words;

Experience isn't passive, it's creative. Since our inner experience is created by us, it can and will change as soon as we change our thinking.

It works like this for everyone, even when it doesn't look like it works this way. We are all walking around in our own mentally created reality, informed by our psychology, where our own preconceived ideas and expectations (which we might also call beliefs) shape our experience of any given situation.

This doesn't mean that what you're perceiving is not 'real'.

I once had the privilege of working with a couple of clients with phantom limb pain. Whilst they were missing a limb, both of them experienced a sense of pain in the limb that was no longer there. The pain was real, but it was generated in their mind, not in the limb. Amazingly, the more they understood the true nature of perceiving this pain, the less they experienced the pain.

This again points to how our mind really works. Just like we are feeling the pain of a limb that isn't actually there, we can experience the anxiety of something bad happening that isn't happening, other than in our mind. We can experience anything that we think about because our minds are so powerful.

Imaginal things look real to us because they are real in our consciousness. But that doesn't mean they're actually real, outside. We sometimes think we have a problem until we stop thinking about it, and our whole experience transforms. The potential outside our awareness is huge, and most of us are only aware of a tiny fraction of it.

Most of us, most of the time, are using our minds innocently and unconsciously, creating things we don't really want to create. But when we learn more about how it works, we can begin to create more of what we want, and less of what we don't want, releasing more potential and higher performance.

WHY CHANGE IS POSSIBLE

The reason it's possible for ten different people to have ten different experiences of the same situation is that 100% of our psychological experience of the outside world is created by us.

I'll pause for a moment...

Perhaps you're thinking: "But what if I'm born into poverty? What if I get hit by a car or somebody punches me in the face? Am I creating that experience?"

Let me be clear. The situation is real. How you think, feel, and eventually act on it is up to you.

If we are feeling stressed in a particular situation and someone else isn't, it's our thinking that does this.

And here's where the freedom comes...

Your inner experience is entirely independent of your circumstances.

If you and I are looking at the same tree, we're not experiencing the same tree. Our experience is 100% subjective. Whilst the tree is made up of the same energy

19

and atoms bouncing around together, we're not experiencing the same tree. In fact, no two people experience the tree in the same way. What you're experiencing is your interpretation of the tree made up by your own past experiences, conditioning, preferences, biases, etc. So when you see the tree, you can't see it independent of your story about it.

'When you change the way you look at things, the things you look at change.'
(Wayne Dyer).

This is a helpful insight to grasp. If we take the example of stress, we can turn our attention away from trying to fix the problem outside ourselves, where we inaccurately think stress is coming from, and instead, understand that we are creating our own psychological experience of stress, which will change as soon as our thinking or awareness changes.

As real as stress feels—and it *is* real for you—it is created by you.

We intuitively know this. Otherwise, 100% of people would feel exactly the same way in every situation.

It's like we are each walking around in our own bubble of reality, interacting with the world and each other, and each assuming that our reality is the correct one. What's more, our personal reality can change in a moment.

We experience our perception as if it's reality, then we have thinking about that perception as if it's a fixed thing. But it isn't fixed. In fact, it's less like stone, and more like soft clay.

Since we create our own psychological experience of life moment-to-moment, anything can change as soon as we choose to change our thinking, or our level of consciousness (we'll cover more of this in chapter 9).

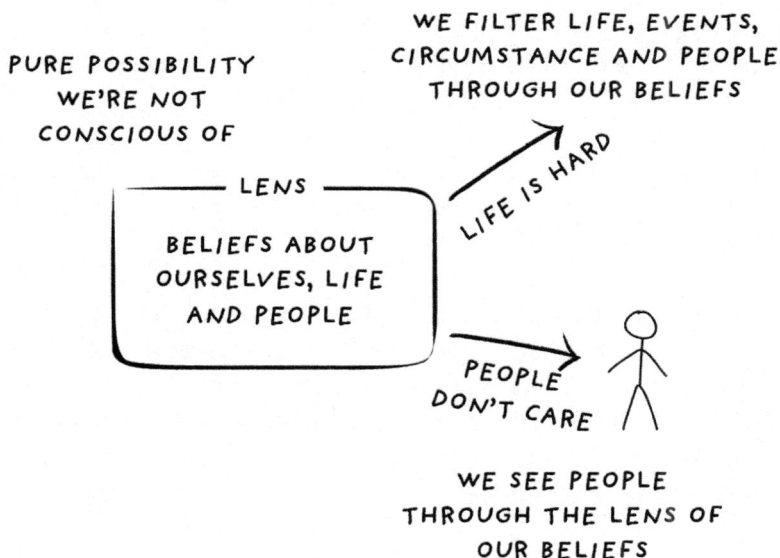

WE FILTER LIFE, EVENTS,
CIRCUMSTANCE AND PEOPLE
THROUGH OUR BELIEFS

PURE POSSIBILITY
WE'RE NOT
CONSCIOUS OF

——— LENS ———

BELIEFS ABOUT
OURSELVES, LIFE
AND PEOPLE

LIFE IS HARD

PEOPLE
DON'T CARE

WE SEE PEOPLE
THROUGH THE LENS OF
OUR BELIEFS

When you truly grasp this understanding, you'll see for yourself that there's a whole world outside of your thinking. We experience a very limited perspective, and we can miss the bigger picture. We're not seeing the truth of things; we're seeing our viewpoint. If you want to change something about your life, then you either need to change your viewpoint, or realise deeply that what you're seeing is simply a perspective.

'In the vastness of the cosmos, everything is going perfectly, but one nasty little thought in your mind can make it a bad day. That is lack of perspective.'
(Sadhguru)

WHAT IF IT'S TRUE?

Admittedly, it can be a challenge to accept what I'm saying.. When I came across this understanding myself, I had to consider: "But what if this is true? What if I really am creating my own experience of life?"

If this understanding feels too radical for you to accept, I'll invite you to consider that simple question for yourself: "What if it's true?"

The thing I love about truth is that if you look hard enough, you'll see it. In fact, you don't have to **learn** truth, you **recognise** it. Usually, when someone properly gets this understanding, it occurs as a deep inner knowing. In a way, the truth is something you've always known; you've just temporarily lost sight of it.

Once I started looking for the truth of how life works, my life started making more sense. I found that I got less upset and more productive. I found I had fewer worries and more confidence because I stopped thinking the limiting thoughts that got in the way of my natural drive to do things.

I realised that when I was thinking of a problem, I was thinking about my thinking. My thinking was the problem, not life, not some external reality, but my perception.

The reason humanity contains such a variety of political viewpoints and orientations, as well as such different religious beliefs or tastes in food, movies, or holiday destinations, is that we each interpret things uniquely.

'There are no facts, only interpretations.'
(Friederich Nietzsche)

You can probably recognise that if you're lying in bed at night feeling anxious, you're creating that experience. At times, I can be so lost in thought about an upcoming meeting that it feels like a shock to me to wake up from my thought-created experience and find myself sitting in bed and not in the meeting. In that example, it's easy to see that 100% of my experience was created by my thinking.

I can also see that I can be in the meeting itself, and be so up in my head that I'm not present with what people are saying, and I'm instead experiencing my own thinking about what they might be thinking, or what might happen.

One time, when I was at home after a very long, busy day at work, I found myself feeling irritated with my kids. I then realised that if I wasn't feeling stressed out with work, I would be having a different experience of them. This did something for me. I realised that I was creating the irritation I was feeling, and when I saw this, I was able to drop it in an instant because I saw through the thoughts and feelings that were creating the irritation. Another way of saying this is that I was able to drop it because I saw that my kids weren't being inherently irritating, but that I was being irritable.

If this sounds subtle, it's not. It's like two different worlds. One where things just are. And one where you see that you're creating your own experience of the things in your consciousness.

In other words, we see life through the lens of our beliefs. Everything we hear, feel and experience is tinted (and at times entirely created) by the power of our mind.

Everything that you are conscious of is your own psychology. This is an inside-out understanding. That is explained in both science and spirituality. I would call it a psycho-spiritual understanding of life.

REFLECTION

Where in your own life can you see that you are creating your own psychological experience? For example, when you last got upset, how much can you see it was because of your thinking, not the event itself?

How far does this understanding extend for you? Where in your life can you not see that you're creating your own experience, and things just look fixed?

What would change for you if you saw that you are creating 100% of your psychological experience?

BETWEEN PSYCHOLOGY AND SPIRITUALITY

Every spiritual teacher I've ever studied speaks about consciousness, so what if there is a spiritual component to understanding how we work as human beings?

During my studies in psychology, I also studied Buddhism, and I was often pleasantly surprised by how I consistently found both fields crossed over with very little conflict. It was therefore no surprise to me when the NHS started to adopt the Eastern practice of mindfulness to help people with their wellbeing.

Whether we study the psychology of perception, neuroception, neuroscience, the observer effect in quantum physics, or spirituality, there's a lot of different things all pointing towards the same truth:

We create our experience of life from the inside-out.

We all experience life differently because of our psychology. This inside-out understanding accounts for every individual difference, as well as all of our collective experiences. It is the reason there are people in extreme poverty who have more peace, security of mind, and joy than certain multi-millionaires. It's the reason you can go to bed thinking your life is a nightmare, and then wake up wondering what on earth you were thinking because you've woken up to a new perspective.

We experience our thinking as if it were real, and we live in a moment-to-moment psychological experience of our lives.

Author and lecturer Sydney Banks understood this at the deepest level. In 1974, he experienced what we might call a spontaneous enlightenment. He woke up to how the human experience truly works.

Many different spiritual teachers will talk about the spiritual world and the human world, or the formless and the form. Sydney Banks said that the link between these two worlds is thought. He further went on to describe three principles that create the human experience:

UNIVERSAL CONSCIOUSNESS

Due to Universal Consciousness, we each have the ability to be aware of our experience. Consciousness is like a blank screen, and we see our thinking on this screen of awareness. Universal Consciousness is the same for you as it is for me, and shows up in each of us as our own awareness of what we are experiencing moment-to-moment.

UNIVERSAL THOUGHT

The ability to think comes from the power of what Sydney called universal thought. Universal Thought is the tool we use to create our own experience of life. Since thought is energy, it is completely fluid and changeable at any moment. The power of Universal Thought shows up in each of us. We just use it differently to create different experiences in life. The fact that each of us can have a different perspective is due to the power of thought.

UNIVERSAL MIND

Sydney defined Universal Mind as the intelligent energy of life. Some people call it life force, spirit, nature, chi, God, or the force. I just call it the magic of life itself. Universal Mind shows up in all of us as our own natural intelligence, which helps us navigate life.

These three principles are constantly working in the background, in each of us, allowing us to either consciously or unconsciously create our own unique experience in and of life. This means that we each have the same tools for living, but that we simply choose to use them differently.

I've found that there's no depth to how much I can see this understanding for myself. The more I look towards how I'm creating my own experience of life, the more I see, and the more I feel like I'm waking up.

As Sydney says:

'It's nothing new. It's something that's been in this reality since the beginning of time, and it's called Truth. And Truth is a spiritual intelligence, before the formation of this reality we know.

How do you get to this Truth? How does it become alive?

It's really very simple.

The Three Principles that bring everything into creation... Divine Mind, Divine Consciousness and Divine Thought. And with Mind, Consciousness and Thought to guide you through life, you learn to use them properly.

Now you don't really have to think about Mind because Mind is the intelligence of all things. You've already got it. Consciousness makes you aware. You're already aware. What's left is Thought, and Thought is like the rudder of a ship; it guides you through life. And if you can learn to use that rudder properly, you can guide your way through life way, way better than you ever imagined.

You can go from one reality to another. You can find your happiness. And when illusionary sadness comes from memories, you don't try to figure them out; please don't try to do that, you'll get yourself in trouble.

All you have to do is simplicity again, is realize that it is Thought. The second you realize it's thought, it's gone. You're back to the now, you're back to happiness.

So, don't get caught up in a lot of details. In this world, the smaller it is, the more powerful it is. And here we have Mind, Consciousness and Thought. That's very simple. That's the answer.'

(Sydney Banks)

Whilst spiritual teachers use words like formless, emptiness, space, and nothingness, as a transformative coach, I like to use words like possibility, potential, freedom, and transformation. But we're all talking about the same thing, the essential truth that...

There's a whole world of possibility outside of your current thinking. And you can touch that space of freedom, and live your life from it.

IMPLICATIONS

If you're not conscious of how this works, you can go your whole life assuming that you see life just the way it is. But you're not built that way. We don't see life as it is. You're seeing life through your own psychology. And how you see things is never fixed. It is always changeable.

We live in a moment-to-moment psychological experience. How we perceive the world is a reflection of our own programmed, habitual thinking. Then, out of how we see the world, we think, feel and act, leading to the results we see in life.

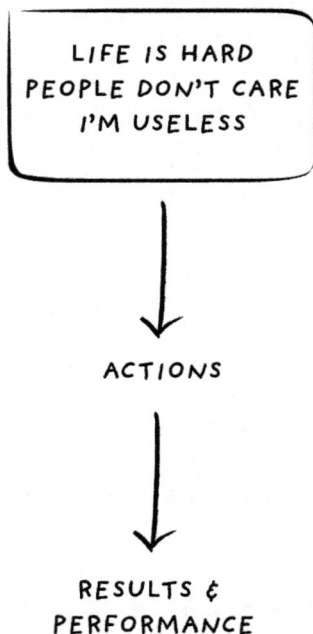

```
┌─────────────────────┐
│   LIFE IS HARD      │
│ PEOPLE DON'T CARE   │
│   I'M USELESS       │
└─────────────────────┘
          │
          ▼
      ACTIONS
          │
          ▼
    RESULTS &
   PERFORMANCE
```

We each filter life and events through our own conditioning and our thinking, which means that we experience a limited perspective. This means that the way we experience our self-image, our emotions, other people, and life itself is all via thought.

The good news is that this means that all of your experience is completely changeable.

In his best-selling book *Man's Search For Meaning*, the survivor of three German concentration camps, Viktor Frankl, describes how he could find moments of peace and joy in the midst of some of the worst conditions imaginable. The reason he was able to do this is that he, like all of us, created his own psychological experience. And if Viktor Frankl can do this in a concentration camp, we can do it too.

The rest of this book will help you see the implications of this understanding in your life and point you in the direction of finding more freedom, happiness, peace, and possibility.

KEY INSIGHTS:

◆ We don't experience life as it is. We think that we observe one objective reality, but this isn't true. We experience life through various filters or lenses, shaped by our own personal psychology. And our psychology is mostly created by our previous experiences.

◆ We're living in a psychological reality, not a physical one. In other words, we're actually experiencing our psychology rather than a physical reality directly.

◆ You don't have to change your mind to see the truth, you realise the truth.

◆ You can change your experience by either changing your thinking or seeing that it's thinking/a perspective.

◆ Everyone's perceptions are different, even if we are looking at the same object or situation.
◆ There's more out there that's possible beyond your personal thinking.

FROM INSIGHT TO ACTION

(A prompt to implementing the insights in this chapter):

If it's true that you really are creating your own psychological experience of life and circumstance, what would change for you in how you live your life, your relationships, your work?

CHAPTER 2

POSSIBILITY

*'There is freedom waiting for you, on the breezes
of the sky. And you ask, "What if I fall?" Oh, but
my darling, "What if you fly?" '*
Erin Hanson

If it's true that we create our own experience of life, what's
there before we start creating?

The answer is *possibility*.

Most people don't talk about possibility. In fact, if we're
not careful, we can forget about it. But possibility is what
we all desire to live into. It's what we are all built for, and
it's what we were born into.

I remember my first ever romantic relationship and being
in love for the first time. I recall skipping down the street in
feelings of infatuation and giddiness, singing!

The reason I was so excited is because of the possibility of the potential future we might have. I thought, "This is the one!" And I imagined living happily ever after.

Perhaps when you start a new job, you might find yourself incredibly present, engaged, and alive. It's because you're excited about the possibility this new job creates, the idea that it could be the place where all your skills and experience come to fruition, where you will finally be recognised for your many talents.

The vision of what *could be* gives us zest, meaning, and aliveness. Children have a sense of possibility in bucketfuls, and I believe that possibility is what we all want to return to, to step outside our fears and doubts and into a world of fuller potential.

As a kid, I remember watching one of the early Superman films where Clark Kent is practically an adult when he discovers he possesses the ability to fly. Until then, it had never occurred to him to even try (why would it?). Can you imagine going your entire life with the ability to fly and never discovering it? It makes me wonder if we all have our own version of this.

Whether you dream of starting your own business, pursuing an athletic career, or following your heart in music, many of us paint over that sense of possibility with a set of limiting beliefs. Most of us aren't living into possibility. We're living into limitation.

Imagine not following your passion or desire to start a business in case it fails. This is an example of living into limitation.

Now imagine going on a first date because, despite what your anxious thinking might tell you, this person might be your future spouse. This is possibility.

We can each move from a limited perspective to a life of pure possibility. When we see outside the box of our limiting beliefs, we realise there's more available to us than we'd ever thought possible.

One thing to realise is that we don't need to try to think positively to create possibility for ourselves. Possibility is already there underneath the thinking we have that gets in the way.

INNATE POTENTIAL

Babies are born inherently free. For them, life is pure potential, opportunity, and possibility.

If we're born inherently free, with pure possibility in front of us, why don't we feel this way? What changed?

I'm going to tell you the answer...

Nothing.

Nothing changed.

You just started thinking that certain things weren't possible for you.

Perhaps someone told you that you will never amount to anything, or maybe you were given the message that your needs were not as important as other people's, or media messaging tells you that you're not attractive.

Based on these experiences, you started deciding what kind of person you were and what was, and wasn't possible for you. You made decisions about life and people and formed ideas on how you would navigate life... based on those beliefs.

And here's the secret:

Those beliefs aren't true. They are made of thought.

As soon as you see this for yourself, you'll be stepping into a world of pure possibility where you can follow your heart and live the life you'd love to live.

'When you have exhausted all possibilities, remember this - you haven't'
(Thomas Edison)

We're all, in fact, living in a world of pure possibility and potential, but what we see is limitation. You needn't create possibility; it is already there underneath the self-created world you've scribbled over with your thinking.

So, rather than try to get to a place of possibility, your only job is to see that everything already is possible. You just have a veil of thought clouding it. You're already free to live the life you desire; you're just telling yourself you're not free to.

When you were a young child, you could dream about what you wanted to be when you grew up. Then one day you started to get a fixed idea of who you were and what was possible, and you stopped fantasising, and started being what you thought was practical. Chances are, what you thought was practical was just you stepping into a survival mode.

Rather than follow your passions, you decided to follow where the money is, or do whatever you needed to do to fit in and get along.

You stopped following your heart. You started following what you 'should' do, what you 'needed' to do.

One of the things I love about my kids is that, at their young age, they have very little self-consciousness, and therefore no idea of limitation. As far as they're concerned, they can grow up to be whatever they want to be, whether that's an astronaut, a racing car driver, a princess, or something else entirely.

What's more, they have no concerns about fitting in, being accepted, or not being loved. Yet as we grow, we feel ourselves contained in the imaginal 'box'; we start to think that we need to do more than what we were previously doing in order to be loved and accepted.

Usually, from the moment we begin to believe our limiting perspectives, we start redefining who we are and adapting our behaviour to fit in, please people and make it through life. We go from being completely open and fluid, to believing that we're in some way inadequate. We then unconsciously begin looking through the lens of insecurity, and we fear rejection.

THE BLANK SCREEN OF POSSIBILITY

I think of possibility like a blank screen that you can then create on top of. We habitually create limitation on top of this blank screen of pure possibility. The brilliant thing is that whatever you put on top of this screen, it still remains blank underneath.

Just as you can wipe a whiteboard clean at any moment if you don't like what you've drawn, you can do the same with your limiting beliefs as soon as you see through them.

INFINITE POSSIBILITY AND
PURE POTENTIAL

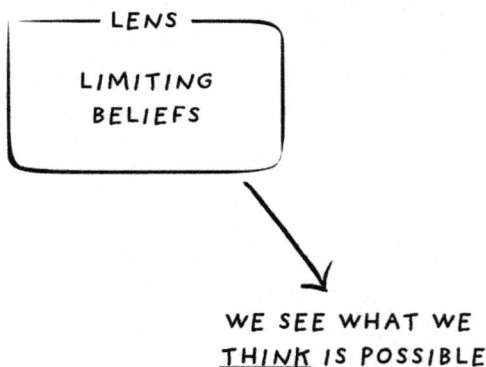

———— LENS ————

LIMITING
BELIEFS

WE SEE WHAT WE
THINK IS POSSIBLE

Even if you paint your screen with stories of anxiety, self-deprecating thoughts, or negative thinking, the good news is that you can erase it all in a single swipe and go back to the blank screen of endless possibility. (More on this in chapter 8, but for now, let's explore this blank screen of possibility).

LIFE THROUGH A LENS

We don't see what's possible; we see what we *think* is possible.

What if you're not as open-minded as you think you are? As much as it looks like we're looking at life, events and people as they are, we're already filtering those things through our beliefs.

We're continually filtering everything through the lens of judgment, evaluating whether things fit in with our reality.

This filtering includes whether it is good or bad for us, whether we like or dislike something, etc. This lens is our world view, a self-perpetuating limited reality, reinforced by confirmation bias, until it becomes a self-fulfilling prophecy, (more on this shortly). We can't stop this lens, but we can observe it, see it, and dis-identify from it when we see that it's not who we are.

Transformative coaches like myself talk about being limitless and living into pure possibility and full potential. This is because when we see past our limited thinking, we really do feel limitless.

It's not uncommon for people who have worked with me to say, "I really can do anything I want to do and be anyone I want to be", because they see past their thought-created limitations. They really do see pure possibility and limitless potential.

WE DON'T SEE THINGS AS THEY ARE

I used to teach mindfulness, and I used to find that one of the limitations of mindfulness is assuming that by practising meditation, you are more present with the way things are.

After years of mindfulness, I found myself still stuck with many of the same problems and patterns in my life. In short, I struggled with anxiety because I continually believed that either something was wrong with me, or something was wrong out there in life. I was living in an almost constant state of hypervigilance, which again, I could be present with, but nothing really changed.

The reason I didn't notice any transformations was because I mistakenly believed I was being present with a real fixed thing. In other words, I thought I was being present with something independent of my thinking, but this wasn't true. As far as I was concerned, life really was hard, so my being present with it didn't actually help.

The reason I stayed stuck was because I inaccurately assumed that I was being present with life, anxiety, people, or situations. I didn't realise that my experience was coming from me. I thought that my experience of life was coming from life. When in fact, it was being created by my own personal psychology and the things I was thinking about, were created by me. Because here's how it really works;

You don't look at something with bare attention. You can't. You look at it through thought. Through a lens.

I came to see that we're not relating to life and situations; we're relating to our thinking. In other words, you think you're relating to something objectively, but you're not; you're relating to your thinking about it.

What we see is filtered through our beliefs, conditioning, and expectations.

CONFIRMATION BIAS

Our beliefs, expectations, interpretations and descriptions of life all come from our memories of the past. They shape what we see and, therefore, how we relate to the present moment.

For example, if you go and buy a particular make and model of car, the chances are you will start noticing how many other models of that car there are.

We recently bought a new camper van. After we'd bought it, my wife exclaimed on more than a few occasions how "everyone's got a camper van!"

I have two theories about that. Either there suddenly became more camper vans on the road, or she was now seeing them because she was looking for them.

Another example is if you believe that your political view is the correct one, you will see things that confirm this and ignore things that disconfirm it.

For me, it seems like we're all looking out at life through the various lenses, or filters, that we've inherited along the way. If you've developed the belief that 'life is hard', then you'll be looking at life through that lens. Alternatively, if you've been conditioned to believe that 'life is a playground', then you'll have a very different experience of life.

The lenses you've inherited become your world view, and because it's unconscious, you have no idea that you're looking through it. This lens leaves us somewhat closed-minded and relates any information via what we already know, meaning that all information is tainted by past opinion.

Often, when we learn something, we mostly learn through assimilation. We assimilate when we modify information coming at us to fit in with what we already know and how we already see things. So we make up stuff in our minds, such as "I'm not good enough", so when something contrary to that happens, we discount it to make it fit. We shape experiences to fit in with our pre-existing beliefs.

Another process through which we learn is called *accommodation*. This is where we change what we know to fit new information. This learning process is still limited as we unconsciously compare new information to what we already think we know.

Sometimes we dismiss information because it doesn't fit our way of seeing things.

When we talk with someone with a different opinion, we may dismiss what they say, get upset, angry, or defensive. Rather than toy with and see their reality, we shut off and don't listen fully. Consider that this is our ego wanting to be correct.

We make sense of our world through a meaning-making mind. An interesting take on this is that most of our habitual thoughts are actually an attempt to justify a decision that we've already made about life leaving us close-minded.

SELF-FULFILLING PROPHECY

In the way that I've described here, our past creates our future. We can literally predict how someone will think and act in the future, unless they step out of their habitual way of being.

Beliefs influence our actions, and these actions or inactions can lead to results and consequences that confirm our beliefs. For example, imagine you believe you won't pass a job interview, so you don't study for it. This might lead you to go to the interview underprepared and overly nervous, and it might result in you not getting the job.

At this stage, it is important to remember that our beliefs and biases go on top of the blankness, possibility and openness, and that the possibility is still always there.

REFLECTION

Given that we live in a world of pure possibility, what are the beliefs and thoughts you tend to put on top of that possibility with your habitual thinking?

When have you lived into the pure potential and possibility of creating something in your life?

Where in your life are you living into limitation?

What are you making more important: limitation or possibility?

DRIFTING THROUGH LIFE

It's so easy to habitually live into a life of limitation. Instead of living a life of pure potential and possibility, the autopilot survival mode runs the show, where most of our actions are, in fact, reactions. We thereby live into a kind of default future based on our limited beliefs. The result is that we can end up drifting through life without ever realising it.

People don't tend to create; they tend to react, thereby living into a habitual future.

If you have a fear of public speaking now, the chances are you'll have a fear of public speaking in the future, too. We tend to drag our problems around with us, creating more of the same patterns in our lives. That is, unless we wake up from the thoughts that create these patterns.

One of the signs that we're on autopilot is that we might say "always", "never" (for example: "I always get overlooked for sports teams!" or "I've never been good at anything"). When true possibility presents itself, life feels unfamiliar, and people get scared. The comfort zone is really a zone of familiarity where your life has already been written ("I always do this or that, so… I'll always do this or that!").

You're creating your experience of life, but most people create from their pasts, which isn't creating, it's reacting.

One of my clients, Kate came to me because she wanted to understand more about how her psychology worked and how it was impacting her life. She knew she was holding herself back and that more was possible; she just couldn't quite see it.

Kate owned her own business and had several people working for her. It was a mostly successful company, but they were going through a tricky period and were at a financial loss.

A few of her employees had approached her, raising concerns about a member of staff who they would often see on their phone during working hours, and consistently doing the bare minimum while other employees struggled with their workload. Kate found this almost impossible to deal with as she had a continued avoidance of conflict. What was most interesting to me was that we never directly discussed this in our sessions until she came in one day and told me that she had fired the employee.

Kate: I just realised something.

Chris: What's that?

Kate: "I can't handle conflict" is a thought.

Chris: That's right.

Kate: I thought that was just real! Now I see it was just in my head!

Due to the fact that Kate had learnt more about how her mind works, she saw through the illusion of her thinking (specifically that "I can't handle conflict" was a thought, and not the truth). In the process, she also realised that she had unconsciously been pretending that the employee's misconduct hadn't been happening.

With this clarity, she then took what she thought was the necessary action to address the underperforming employee.

She was living in a thought-created reality where she couldn't handle conflict, looking out at life through this false lens.

Imagine if you were similarly living in a reality where you couldn't do x-y-z. It probably wouldn't even occur to you to try.

There is so much possible for us that we can't see because of our assumptions that we're 'not good at conflict', 'not good enough', 'not creative enough', or simply 'not able to do that'. When you see beyond that thinking, doorways you didn't even know were there, begin to appear.

You're looking out at life through your thinking, which means that you're not really seeing the pure possibility of life; instead, you're seeing your own limited possibilities, often through the lens of anxiety.

UNCERTAINTY

The truth is that the future is pure possibility. Yet we don't see it as that. We create our ideas for our future in the here and now with limited imagination.

Recently, another client, Tom, told me he was scared of the future. I was feeling particularly present at the time, and asked him, 'How can you be scared of the future?'

Tom: Well, I mean I'm scared of the uncertainty.

Chris: But that's like you saying you're scared of nothing. The future doesn't exist, and so it is nothing. The future is empty. The uncertainty you're talking about is like a blank screen, and I know you're not telling me you're scared of the blank screen. In order for you to be feeling scared, how must you be looking at that blank screen?

Tom: I'm assuming that something bad is going to happen.

Chris: And what would happen if we take away the thought of something bad happening?

Tom: I'd feel free.

Tom again: But isn't that just made up? The idea of removing that thought?

Chris: Is it any more made up than the thought of something bad happening? One thought creates stress and struggle, and one creates freedom.

Tom: Oh, yeah!

Chris: What do you think the difference is between uncertainty and pure possibility?

Tom: I don't know?

Chris: Nothing. It depends on the lens you're looking through. The future is empty. We imagine with thought, and then we feel that thinking. Uncertainty is blank, not scary. The future is full of pure possibility, and we paint it with our thinking and then experience that thinking.

We keep ourselves small with our limited thinking, and we hold ourselves back from being our natural brilliance. Since we get in our own way, we experience a pervasive and lasting feeling of discontent because we're not following our potential, which I would say is what we're here for. We have a deep knowing that there's more that is possible for us, but we're so busy trying to survive and get through life that we miss life itself.

The key is to see this for yourself and see through your limiting beliefs to the innate potential inside yourself and the inherent possibility available in life.

PUSHING AWAY POSSIBILITY

We might sometimes get into a situation that doesn't quite fit with how we see things. You might get offered a promotion you weren't expecting, or get asked on a date by someone you think is too good for you.

At times like these, we might push away the possibility because it feels uncomfortable or unfamiliar. This is when we say things like "I can't believe it". Or "I can't believe this has happened to me, I don't deserve it!".

If you ever find yourself saying, "I can't believe this amazing thing has happened to me", it might be because it doesn't fit into your thought-created reality.

If we're not careful, we can end up pushing this amazing thing away, and we might call this self-sabotage.

An example of this is if you get into a relationship with someone you think is better than you. As far as you're concerned, you're not good enough for this person. So you unconsciously push this person away with your actions, and inactions, and end up creating a self-fulfilling prophecy of; "I told you! I knew I wasn't good enough for them".

I once had a client hire me to help them break their pervasive cycle of procrastination. They were finding that they were putting off more and more in their life, and the side-effect was that they were feeling unfulfilled.

We rarely got to have an actual coaching session because they kept putting off their appointments to see me. At a certain stage, I pointed this out to them and they saw the pattern for themselves. By naming it, we were able to deal with it directly and get to the root cause of their inaction so that it didn't play out in their life anymore.

Self-sabotage shows what you think of yourself and your world. You decline or push away an opportunity that would enrich your life when you think you don't deserve it, reinforcing what you think of yourself. When something doesn't resonate with what we think and feel about ourselves, we say we don't deserve it and push it away.

If you think something is possible for other people, but not for you, there's a chance that you're pushing away that possibility. Because remember;

There is possibility, and you're putting your thinking on top of it.

In the next chapter, we'll look at how much we put *on top of* possibility with our thinking.

KEY INSIGHTS

◆ We create limitations over and on top of possibility, and we create those limitations with thought (specifically, what we call limiting beliefs).

◆ You don't need to create possibility; it is already there underneath the self-created world you've painted with your thinking.

◆ You don't have to live into your default habitual future, you can break free as long as you rise your level of awareness above it.

◆ So much is possible outside of your limited thinking.

FROM INSIGHT TO ACTION

If it was true that you were living in a world of pure possibility, limited only by your personal thinking and not your circumstance, what would be the very next step you might take towards creating a life you'd love?

CHAPTER 3

WHAT ARE YOU ADDING TO IT?

'Thought creates our world, and then says "I didn't do it".'
David Bohm

Our brain is like a supercomputer for adding meaning and stories to life. The more we see the truth of this, the freer we are. I remember the very first time I saw this for myself.

I'd just come out of a relationship and was feeling lost, anxious and depressed. I'd broken up with my partner and was devastated and in a lot of emotional pain.

A friend of mine recommended that I get away on a mindfulness retreat at a place she'd visited herself. I had practised a little mindfulness before, and being one to dive in at the deep end, I booked my place at the retreat centre in just a few days' time, without knowing anything much about it.

I arrived for my week-long stay at the retreat centre and was soon introduced to the schedule. There would be three hours of sitting meditation per day, and extended periods of silence. It soon dawned on me that I would be completely alone with my feelings. What had my friend gotten me into?

I was going through one of the hardest periods of my life, and she'd told me to go somewhere where there were no distractions: no mobile phones, no TV to numb myself with, no music, no alcohol, and not a single drop of caffeine. Not only did I need to be alone in my despair and loneliness, but I also needed to detox from coffee! Safe to say, I made a mental note to have some strong words with my 'friend' as soon as I got my phone back.

The first few days were tough. I had honestly never felt my own feelings so much in my life. I was very close to leaving the retreat a few days in, when a zen master came in to lead us through a guided meditation.

From his intense gaze to his slow, considered demeanour and warm smile, I immediately felt I was in the presence of somebody much more wise than myself. Given that I felt so devastated and broken at the time, I decided to sit with my feelings and surrender to whatever wisdom he might have. I had nothing to lose.

When we got the opportunity to ask him a question, I enquired, "I'm just out of a relationship, going through a breakup, and it hurts so much, what can I do to ease the pain?"

He gazed at me.

It was more like he gazed through me, in fact, into the deepest part of me. What he said to me, gave me goosebumps.

After what seemed like minutes, but was perhaps only a few seconds, he asked me, "What are you adding to it?"

Now, I don't know what anyone else in that room heard, but in a single moment, I saw all the meaning that I had been adding to the situation.

And then I witnessed it dissolve right before me.

What came to mind was this:

I'll never find love again
I've ruined my life
I'm broken
I've ruined her life
I'm a bad person
I'll never be happy again
Something's wrong with me

It all appeared in my mind, and I saw it for what it was. Thought. Story. A narrative. Meaning. All created by my own mind. And none of it fundamentally true.

In the same moment I saw it, I saw through the fictitious nature of it, and the thought faded, along with all the emotional anguish I was feeling.

My body started flowing with energy. I felt as light as a bird. I sensed tears gathering in my eyes at what I can only describe as a feeling of coming home. The deep peace and aliveness started reverberating around my body immediately and continued for days. I was free.

I don't remember many of the details of the rest of the retreat. But I do recall periods of pure joy, belly laughing, and more presence than I ever recall experiencing in my life. At some point towards home time, I realised that I had been having almost no thinking for the last few days. When I got my phone back, I immediately texted my friend and asked if I could take her out to lunch to thank her.

Life has never been the same for me since. I've never forgotten what that zen teacher said to me, and I often find myself asking the very same question: "What am I adding to it?" whenever I'm feeling upset, down, stressed, or in some way unsettled. As soon as I see through the story, I find myself in a deep place of peace and presence.

'Man is troubled not by events, but by the meaning he gives to them.'
(Epictetus)

CIRCUMSTANCE AND THE MEANING WE ADD TO IT

In the example I've just given, I was not experiencing life directly. I was experiencing my story of it; "I'll never find love again. I've ruined my life", and so on. Due to the way my psychology was working, I contaminated the event - the break-up I was going through - with my personal assumptions, and I genuinely believed this was simply the way things were. I failed to see the separation between my thoughts and reality.

There's a situation, event, or circumstance, and there's our personal thinking. These are two independent domains. But they don't get experienced by us as independent. They get experienced by us as one and the same. In other words, by the time we are aware of something, we've already had thinking about it.

We think we're being conscious of an event, or an object, when really what we're conscious of, is our thinking, or perception about the event or object.

In order to begin to see this for yourself, you need a shift in consciousness. You need to raise your awareness to see what is thought, and what is not thought. It has helped me, and many of my clients, to look at this visually.

Let's take the example of a person being made redundant:

Situation	Thought (what we add to it, or what we make it mean)
Made redundant at work	I'm a failure I'll never find a good job again Why me? Life is unfair I'm incompetent What's wrong with me?

In my psychology training, as much as I hated the statistics modules, one of the most helpful things I learnt was that causation is often confused with correlation. In other words, things we think are tied together often aren't. Practically, what that means for us, is that our experience is **independent** of circumstances. If you can see the separateness of the situation from your thinking, you will have a lot more peace and freedom in your life.

Here's a real example a client of mine shared with me:

Situation	Thought (what we add to it, or what we make it mean)
My niece doesn't want to do A-levels.	I have not been a good enough role model. She probably doesn't see me as someone to help/mentor her. It will be my fault if she struggles in life. I failed her as an aunt. I'm not good enough.

We feel our thinking of what we're adding to the situation, not the situation.

What follows is an old Taoist parable that I think illustrates the power of the meaning we can add to events. When I first heard this, I was shocked at the perspective that the story points towards. This is one of the most freeing stories I have ever heard, and honestly, my life has been a lot easier with the insights it offers:

There is a story of a wise old farmer who owned a farm with his wife and son. They did not have many animals, but they did own a horse, which they had saved long and hard to buy.

One day, the horse ran away. "How terrible, what bad luck", said the neighbours.

The farmer replied, "Bad luck? Good luck? Who knows?"

Sometime later, the horse returned from the hills, bringing with him several wild mares. "What marvellous luck", said the neighbours.

"Good luck, bad luck, who knows?" replied the farmer.

The son began to tame one of the wild horses, but one day he was thrown off and broke his leg. "What bad luck," said the neighbours.

"Good luck, bad luck, who knows?" replied the farmer.

The next week, the army came to the village to take all the young, able-bodied men to war. When they saw the farmer's son with his broken leg, they let him off.

Now was that good luck or bad luck?

Who knows?

(Taoist Parable)

When I fully grasped the intention of this story myself, I let go of the assumptions I had about what is right or wrong, or good and bad.

I had no idea that this level of freedom existed until I really took this in and applied it in my own life. If we tell ourselves that something is bad, we feel bad. If we tell ourselves that we don't know how things will ultimately work out for us, we feel more at ease and free with life.

I am deeply moved by the story of one of my clients who told me how they were once stung by a hornet whilst out on a relief mission in the Panama jungle. Because of the hornet sting and resulting anaphylaxis, she was sent to Bogotá to assist a man in charge of organising the Colombian phase of the expedition. The rest, as they say, is history - they were married less than a year later and eventually had two children, all thanks to the hornet!

We can judge external situations, but ultimately, we never know how things are going to turn out. It would seem obvious that certain things in life are just plain wrong or bad, like, for example, being stung by a hornet. Or are they?

REFLECTION

What meaning are you adding to a recent situation that you've been upset about?

What might happen for you if you separated the meaning from the situation? How might you then feel? What might you then do?

What in your life have you assumed was bad for you, only for it to later look and feel entirely different?

When I ask myself these questions, I start to become more conscious, more aware. I start to experience life with less thought and more presence. I love reminding myself that I don't know the bigger picture of life. So many times, something has happened that I think is bad, and it's later turned out to be the best thing that could have happened for me, just like my relationship breakup. I had assumed that it was a bad thing, but now I see it very differently, especially since I now have children I love with all my heart with another woman, my wife.

A PSYCHOLOGICAL EXPERIENCE OF LIFE

The earlier example of being made redundant came from a real client of mine. The client was taking the redundancy personally, that it was because they were incompetent, and that it was useless trying to get another job because of this. In their mind, they were simply lucky to have landed the job in the first place; it was just a fluke, and they were now "screwed".

At one point in our coaching session together, I too got caught up in their story of the redundancy and their own so-called incompetence. But then I remembered that situations are contaminated with thought.

Inside his thought-created reality, the situation really was quite worrying, it seemed. But my own feeling of hopelessness for the client quickly alerted me to the fact that I had started to buy into his reality of incompetence. When I came back to myself, I had the sense to ask him how many other people were made redundant.

"Five hundred", he replied.

I'd assumed it was just him, or a handful of people that were made redundant. Any hopelessness I had for him faded in an instant, and within minutes it had faded for him too, as soon as he saw that the redundancy had nothing to do with any incompetence on his part.

We mistake the nature of what we think is just fixed and true. We superimpose a concreteness onto things which are not concrete. We assume that the things we are conscious of exist independently of our experience, but they don't.

Let's take the example of someone who gets anxious socially:

Alan: I'm nervous about the work party.

Chris: What's the situation you're dealing with in your mind?

Alan: People will look at me and I won't know what to say.

Chris: Why wouldn't you know what to say to someone?

Alan: Because I just wouldn't. I never know what to say.

Chris: You were just telling me about the amazing holiday you've just been on. How did you know what to say then?

Alan: That was different. I wasn't at a party.

Chris: What's the difference in your mind?

Alan: I guess I just overthink at a party and think I'm boring with nothing to say.

Chris: And if you didn't overthink it, and just focused on one conversation with one person at a time, what might that be like?

Alan: I guess it would flow better. But what if I then get nervous?

Chris: What do you think it would be exactly that would make you nervous?

Alan: Not knowing what to say.

Chris: Well, what if it was just the *thought* of you not having anything to say that was making you nervous?

Alan: Yeah, I guess it is just a thought.

Chris: So if you don't focus on that thought, does it still seem like a problem?

Alan: No. It's not there anymore.

The situation in Alan's mind is created by the thought: "What if I don't know what to say?" To him, the situation is that he's boring, uninteresting and has nothing to talk about. The very fear of his social ineptness is likely to lead to a fear of being excluded.

Something happens, and we tell ourselves a story about it. Then that story becomes our reality. Just like Alan, we collapse what happened, with the story we make up about what happened. This is automatic and unconscious, so we don't know we are doing it, and we don't see it. We experience reality and thought as one and the same, as if it is just how it is.

When we see something fixed, or "as is" we are telling ourselves a story. This limits us, and we don't see what is possible because we are confined to a made-up narrative. When we truly see that we are meaning-making machines, we see that what we thought was concrete and real and determined, is just made up of what we created with thought. The deeper we see the truth of how our awareness works along with our thinking, the more things become open and lighter, and we start to see more possibility.

GROUP REALITIES

During my degree in psychology, I was tasked with writing an essay on social constructionism. It was a self-study piece, where we weren't lectured on the subject, but instead were told to study and write about our own insights gained from our research. This was yet another pivotal moment for me, when I realised how much of our world is thought-created.

We're all hallucinating all the time; when we agree about our hallucinations, we call it 'reality'.'
(Anil Seth)

You can think of social constructionism as that which is created, or that which is constructed, due to societal wants and desires, and what is agreed upon. How to act and be, for example, at school, in church, in private members clubs, at family gatherings, in shops, libraries, in the streets, etc.

Without it, society wouldn't function the way it does. What I discovered through my research, is that we have so much group thinking that it creates our society, and unless you actually look, you don't see it as thought-created.

Let's take money, for example.

If I asked you if you'd like one million pounds, no strings attached, you'd probably take me up on the offer. But if I then told you that it was a million pounds in Monopoly money, you'd wonder what use that could possibly be.

So that begs the question, what is money?

Unless you had it in cash, a million pounds would just look like a bunch of numbers on a screen in your bank account. But let's say I gave you a million pounds in banknotes. There, you have the physical paper notes. But that still doesn't actually tell us what money is.

Money is simply an agreed-upon form of exchange. If we stopped agreeing that money meant anything, then it wouldn't mean anything. If an alien came down, or even someone from a distant tribe in another part of the world, and was offered a million pounds, they probably wouldn't be at all interested. This is because they don't buy into our group thinking about the concept of money.

Money is an idea constructed by society. A thought-created thing, which is why any two-year-old will drop the ten-pound note you put in their birthday card just as quickly as they drop the card itself. They don't see the meaning we've assigned to the piece of paper.

Money, or at least our use of it, doesn't exist independent of our thinking. In other words, what use is a million pounds without an agreement? If it's been built using thought, then it's thought-created.

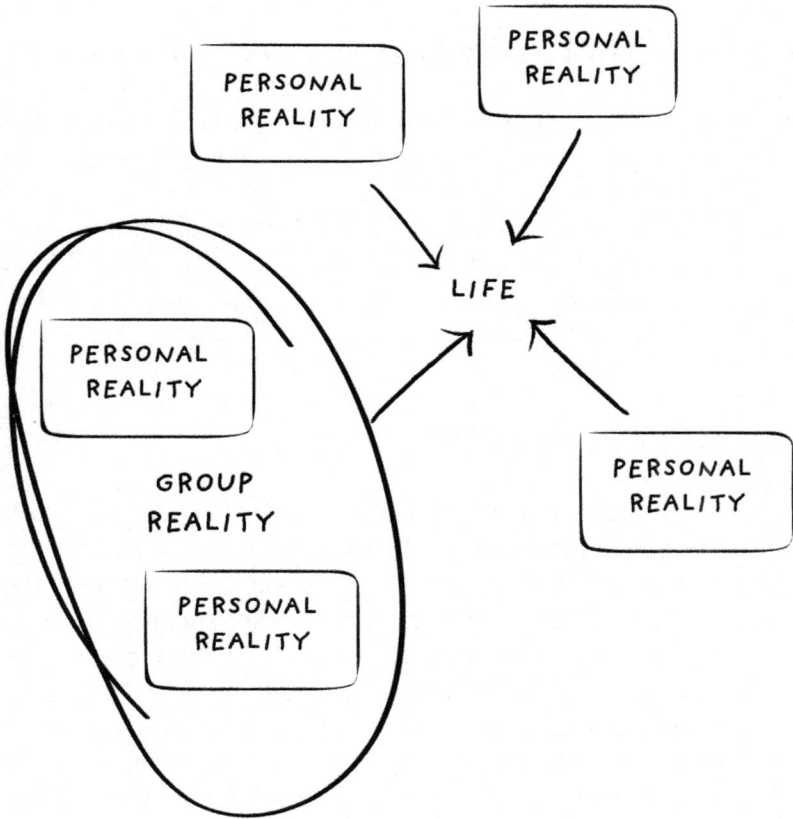

I'm not asking you to take my word for this, I'm inviting you to look for yourself. If you do, you'll see that all the laws we have, our concept of marriage, and even such things as the declaration of a goal when a football crosses the line and hits the back of the net–all these things are created by group thinking and agreed-upon constructs.

Time itself is a construct, broken down into agreed-upon hours, minutes, and seconds.

So what if good, bad, right, or wrong were also constructs?

When I was on a trip to Rome, I toured around the Colosseum. I learnt that approximately 400,000 people had died during its use in the gladiator games. I saw for myself that even the rules we now have around murder are made up. That back in Roman times, it was socially acceptable to throw someone into a situation where they literally had to fight for their lives.

A MATTER OF PERSPECTIVE

When I was a kid, I was watching a nature documentary where I remember part of the programme focused on deer. One scene showed a pack of wolves chasing down and then catching a young deer. The narrator had spent some time introducing us to the family of deer, and the hardships of the mother deer to bring her young into the world and keep them alive. After watching the baby deer for ten minutes, I felt pretty attached to it, and so when a wolf came and did what wolves do, I felt angry and upset. I remember thinking how wrong it was, and; "why can't a wolf eat vegetables or just find an already dead animal?"

More recently, I watched a nature programme, where the focus was on a pack of wolves. Ironically, the narrator painted the story of how hard it is for wolves to survive in the world, with fewer wild pieces of land, and not much to eat, we saw the wolves getting thinner and thinner. The wolves had young, and they were so cute! The narrator explained that if they didn't find food soon, they would surely die. The wolves then came across a herd of deer. When they started chasing them, I found myself willing the wolves to catch just one deer so that they could survive. When they didn't, I found myself tearful at the thought that the young wolves might not make it.

What I realised, was that there is no right or wrong in nature. There is thought that makes things right or wrong, and good or bad. When I'm on the side of the wolf, I want the wolf to catch and eat a deer for their dinner. When I'm focused on the deer, I want the deer to get away. I create for myself what's right and wrong and good and bad. It's a matter of perspective.

'There is nothing either good or bad but thinking makes it so.'
(William Shakespeare)

GOOD LUCK/ BAD LUCK?

We get made redundant, we experience a relationship breakup, or we have a bad meal at a restaurant. If we just let it pass and don't add too much story to it, we bounce back to our natural resilience and wellbeing in no time at all.

One of the things that struck me after the retreat I attended was how the situation, my break-up, hadn't changed at all, but my entire experience had been transformed.

The situation was that I was no longer with my ex, and I lived somewhere else. I still needed to navigate life and the breakup, but I wasn't feeling the despair, hopelessness and anxiety that I had been previously. In its place was a sense of peace and stillness within me. And it hadn't happened over a period of months. It had happened in a single moment. I had stopped adding drama and stories to my life.

This makes perfect sense when you understand how our experience works. Imagine if you're living in a world where you will never find love again, you've ruined your life, and you're broken. How would that feel for you? That's the reality I was living in.

Most of us have experienced a relationship breakup, so we know how much it can hurt. But one thing is true – we don't feel the breakup or the redundancy, we feel our thinking.

When I saw through the illusory nature of my own personal thinking that I was projecting on top of the situation, I no longer felt the feelings of "I'll never be happy again". There was still some hurt, but it felt light. I had been adding so much narrative to the situation, and I didn't even know I was doing it.

What I experienced was a jump in consciousness. The more you look for yourself at the inherent separateness between thought and situations, the more you will wake up from the potential suffering created by a misunderstanding of how it all works, and into more peace and freedom.

KEY INSIGHTS:

◆ We add meaning to life and situations using the power of thought, and we don't see that we're innocently, automatically and almost always unconsciously doing this.

◆ We feel and experience our stories of life, not life itself.

◆ When you raise your level of consciousness, you begin to see more of what's thought-created and what's not.

◆ We experience life separately, and when we agree on what we see, we call it reality.

FROM INSIGHT TO ACTION

Think of a problem or something that's causing you some stress right now in life. What might it be like to drop the stories and narrative that you are adding to it and to act free from them?

CHAPTER 4

PERSONAL REALITY

'The best day of your life is the one on which you decide your life is your own. No apologies or excuses. No one to blame. The gift is yours – it is an amazing journey – and you alone are responsible for the quality of it. This is the day your life really begins.'
Bob Moawad

When I was seven years old, I stepped into a mind-made prison without even knowing that it was me who created it.

I was in class at school, and the teacher was going through the alphabet and asked us to put up our hands if we could think of a word beginning with the letter that she called out.

When she got to G, I put my hand up. She pointed at me and said, "Chris".

"Juggling", I said.

"No, that's J", she replied.

And this is all that happened.

On the inside, however, it was a very different story.

"I'm stupid", I said to myself. "I'm a stupid person".

It was like I'd discovered some truth about myself. Like I'd had a mistaken, dark epiphany. It was a defining moment in my life, because with that thought came a feeling of shame, dread, and a realisation that life would be hard from now on, having discovered that I was stupid.

In that single moment, I pictured myself struggling through life, while everyone else would breeze through it with ease. In my mind, everyone else was "cleverer" than me. In that moment, I saw myself as fundamentally incapable.

It was like my whole world changed in an instant, and I stepped into a new world where:

I'm stupid

Others are more intelligent than me

Life is going to be hard for me

If you were to watch the event back on camera, all that happened was that I made a mistake with the letters G and J. And yet, what happened on the inside would change the course of my life for the next thirty years. It was like stepping into a prison, but at this time, I didn't realise it was only a mind-made prison. I unknowingly began to look at life and circumstance through the lens of "I'm stupid" and "life is hard", thereby creating a life of limitation.

It was an all-encompassing belief that formed the foundation, or basis of my self-created identity.

I really thought that this was just how things were. I honestly believed that this was who I was, and that this was my life. I didn't have any idea that it was my thinking. I didn't realise that I was creating my experience, and that I was innocently and unconsciously creating it with thought. I tied my identity with that belief, not seeing that it was thought and mistakenly believing that it was true.

Going back to chapter three, it looks like this;

Situation	Thought (what we add to it)
I got a question wrong	*I'm* stupid *Others* are more intelligent than me *Life* is going to be hard for me

BECOMING SELF-CONSCIOUS

Before we start to form our personal reality, we have almost no self-consciousness. In other words, we have very few ideas about who we are. If you observe a three- or four-year-old, they have very little thinking about themselves, leaving them incredibly free to engage with whatever they want. They rarely hold themselves back with negative thoughts (that is, until they learn to think negatively).

Babies aren't born with limiting beliefs. I've never met a toddler who thinks they're not good enough, or worries about being successful. When you look at a young child, there is a sense of presence, freedom, openness, and a natural sense of confidence.

As young children, we don't use our awareness to think much about ourselves until something happens that causes us to do so. Something happens that hurts or causes distress, and because we are egocentric as children, we make it mean something about ourselves, which tends to translate to one of many versions of "not being good enough" as a human being. Prior to this, we live in a space of pure possibility, and as far as we are concerned, we can be anyone we want to be, or do anything we want to do.

From this stress or hurt, we then create an idea of ourselves and of life, and then we live into that idea as if it's reality. It's like there becomes a sticky point in our awareness, where we create and hold onto a belief we have about ourselves. We then identify with that belief and think it's us. Because of these fixed beliefs about life, we create rules and strategies to try to control events so that people don't think badly about us.

OUR PERSONAL REALITY

Our personality, or personal reality, is what creates our very own unique experience of life.

We all have an idea of who we are, which we might call our self-identity. We might say, "This is just who I am", or "that's just my personality". Sometimes this idea of who we are can be really skewed, especially if we build our identity based on our insecurities. The thing is, as soon as you identify with something, you limit yourself to that identity.

Most of us create our sense of self identity unconsciously as a reaction to our experiences. We then sustain our limited viewpoints of ourselves and life by absorbing information that fits in with who we think we are. This then becomes our conditioned self, clouding our natural, authentic being.

Due to the way our psychology works, we end up living in a box, or what I call a mind-made prison, living into a limited and habitual way of being in life.

**INFINITE POSSIBILITY AND
PURE POTENTIAL**

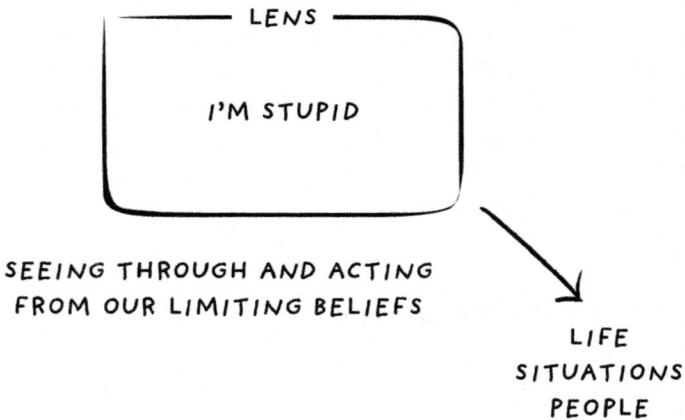

LENS

I'M STUPID

SEEING THROUGH AND ACTING
FROM OUR LIMITING BELIEFS

LIFE
SITUATIONS
PEOPLE

If we think life is hard, we will see things and do things based on this assumption, creating our own self-fulfilling prophecy. I know for myself that when I used to think it was a fact that life was hard, I saw this reflected everywhere I looked because of my way of looking. I would notice the news headlines reflecting threats everywhere, and I focused on the students who were struggling, instead of the students who were thriving.

The good news is that our personal reality is far more pliable than you might realise. Because our personal reality is self-created by our own thinking, our entire experience of ourselves, life, and people is completely malleable.

What if most of what you've been calling you, isn't you at all, but instead just a habitual way you have of thinking about yourself?

SELF-CONSCIOUS IMAGES

It wasn't until I saw the truth of how we create our own personal realities that I woke up from the illusionary belief of "I'm stupid". Once I actually saw on a gut level that "I'm stupid" was a thought, and not who I am, I was free.

Whatever you believe about yourself that hurts, it isn't true; it's a thought, and you can see this for yourself too.

Sometimes we can create an identity based on something that went well for us, and things went our way. Say you acted a particular way and something very positive came from it, you might limit yourself to always being that way.

One of my clients had the identity and belief of always needing to be strong. Whilst they got a lot of benefit from this way of being, they also had some limiting ideas about what being strong meant. They would rarely show their emotions, for example, and wouldn't accept help from anyone, lest they compromise their strong self-image.

Some people might incorrectly label themselves as an "anxious person". But anxiety is an experience of thought and feeling, and not an identity. And yet some people will say, "I'm anxious, it's just who I am". But you're not the emotion of anxiety. If you inaccurately identify with being anxious and then think it's part of your identity, you're fixing and limiting yourself.

Another way of thinking about this is that at times of hurt or stress, we often get self-conscious. In that first moment of becoming self-conscious (often as a child in our formative years), we create an image of how we think others see us. But here's the thing, you need to realise that it's you who draws the image. Not anyone else.

It is important to note that we are often children when we make these potentially life-long decisions about who we think we are. Because we're children, we don't have access to intelligibility, or to all the relevant information to make a decision on who we are and what life is.

Even if someone else does have a negative image of you, it's not you. It's their image, in their minds. If we create an image of ourselves in times of hurt, it's automatically going to be a hurtful image. At a time when we are lacking clarity, we make the worst possible thoughts believable.

We then unconsciously and innocently hold onto these images. Potentially for the rest of our lives. We keep the image in mind, for as long as it takes to realise the truth – that we are not the image we have of ourselves.

'Trauma is not what happened to you, but what happens inside you as a result of what happened to you.'
(Gabor Mate)

LIMITING BELIEFS

In my case, in the mind-made prison of "I'm stupid", I worked harder and longer in my schoolwork than anyone. That is, until I exhausted myself and just surrendered to the belief that I was, in fact, stupid.

Eventually, in my adult life, I burnt out.

It's not surprising when you look at it. I was always the first one in the office and the last one out. I skipped lunch breaks and self-care, all to try to prove to myself and others that I was capable.

I tried thinking positively about being stupid, that I was instead intelligent, but that felt false, like putting a positive thought on top of my reality. The problem was that I still believed that the negative belief was true, and no amount of looking for evidence for and against seemed to shift that belief. In other words, I couldn't see that 'I'm stupid' was a thought.

What I later came to see was that my reality was made of thought, and that the epiphany I had wasn't an epiphany at all. It was an idea I created in a moment of getting a question wrong and having an egocentric seven-year-old brain.

Once I saw this clearly, I no longer needed to challenge the thought because I simply saw that it wasn't true.

This is why positive thinking doesn't work. You don't need to think positively. You just need to see through the illusion of your thinking.

The moment we see through it, we touch the childlike space of possibility that we're inherently born into.

Sometimes when you get to the edge of freedom, you feel nervous. Perhaps you find yourself avoiding something you know would be good for you, or you feel uneasy and you're not sure why. This is actually the edge of your prison, or limiting beliefs, and the other side of the anxiety is freedom.

It could be as you stand up to speak, or as you approach the edge of the swimming pool diving board, or as you go to your romantic partner to initiate a conversation. If you want to know what the edges of your comfort zone are, pay attention to what comes up in your mind when you feel uncomfortable at new opportunities and possibilities. Your discomfort in these situations will show you where you're not free.

Our triggers reveal the walls, or boundaries of our limiting beliefs. They show us the zone of comfort or survival that we create and merely survive within in our lives.

For example, if you live in a world where you're constantly fearful of making mistakes, when you start to break free from this, you're either going to feel very free, or somewhat anxious. Either feeling means you're growing.

If you're not sure what your limiting beliefs are, there's an easy way to find out. Do the things you usually avoid, or don't do something you usually insist on doing. By stopping doing the things that give you comfort, you'll soon see why you do them.

If you're a workaholic, slow down or stop altogether. You'll then see why you do it. You'll come face-to-face with your feelings and the thoughts that create them.

Your prison exists in any place you think you "need" to do something, or "should" do something. There's a mind-made reason for everything you do.

UNCOVERING OUR LIMITING BELIEFS

Before we go on, please recall from the introduction that the intention of this book is to help you clear your mind, not add to it. That being said, this section of the book and the reflections contained in it, are to help you see what's in the way of your clear mind. Just like if you wanted to clear out a room in your house you would have to go through a clearing out process, this part of the book is designed to help you have a spring clean for your mind. If at any times it feels like it's getting more busy or full, please take a break and come back when you feel ready.

We all have our version of believing that we are, on some level, not good enough or inadequate as human beings. But none of us are born believing that we are flawed, broken, or a failure. Something happens that causes us some upset, hurt, or distress, and we make a decision that it means something about us. This is usually some variety of:

I'm not good enough
I'm broken
I'm a failure
I'm not capable
I'm inadequate
I'm wrong
I'm unlikable
I'm worthless

When I was completing my mindfulness teacher training, I recall a small group exercise we were asked to complete that we just couldn't finish. I had to read through a list of negative personal thoughts, just like the ones above, and notice how different thoughts made us feel.

I started reading out the list to my group, and before I was even halfway through the list, one of the group asked me to stop. I looked up from my piece of paper and noticed everyone looked depressed. I felt depressed too. This is the impact of our thinking on our emotions. It hurts. And you don't need to think these hurtful thoughts.

UNDOING OUR FALSE IDENTITY

We form our identity based on who we **think** we are. And who we think we are, comes from past experiences.

Given the fact that experience is what we create in our minds, we can uncreate it just as easily as we create it. As soon as we see the story is a story, we're free. Again, recall that our internal experience is inherently separate from the situation.

REFLECTION

Why do you think you are the way you are, and not another way?

What decisions have you made in the past about who you are?

How do you see yourself? How do you fear you might come across to others?

Now, thinking back to when you might have first formed some of these ideas, images and decisions about yourself, see if you can separate what happened, from what you made it mean about yourself using the table below:

Situation	What you made it mean about yourself

HOW OTHERS LOOK TO US

I used to believe that other people were better than me. When I believed that, I would look up to others and see them as more intelligent, better decision makers, and that they just knew more than I did about navigating life. I was seeing my thinking being reflected back to me.

When I realised it was all a story, it genuinely surprised me to see that no one else seemed to have life figured out either. Our maps of other people might look something like this:

People are untrustworthy
People are cruel
Others don't care
Others are more important than me
Others are better than me
Other people's needs matter more than mine

REFLECTION

How do others look to you?

Try completing the following sentence; Other people are...

WHAT WE THINK ABOUT LIFE

"Life is hard". That's what I thought. And I've had many clients say this to me, too.

Our map of life can look something like this:

Life is hard
The world is scary
Life is not fair
Good things don't happen to me

If we're looking through the lens of "life is hard", we see the things that confirm this hypothesis, and we miss out on the things that don't fit in with our beliefs.

In other words, we experience life as being hard because of our beliefs. But life isn't inherently hard. If it's not inherent in the thing you're looking at, then it's in the way you're looking. (Recall that inherent means that it exists in something as a permanent, essential, or characteristic attribute).

Sometimes it's tricky to see that what we're thinking is creating our personal experience and limiting us. If you're not sure what your personal reality is, consider how life, others, and events look to you. In a way, we see what we're looking for. How things are occurring to you indicates what you're looking for.

Once, early in my career, I was working with a client who, like me earlier in life, believed they were stupid. When I asked them for evidence for that belief, they told me that they only scored 19/20 on a recent test. When I asked what the average score in the class was, they told me it was 17/20.

This is confirmation bias at play again. Once we form our map of the world, we then use that map to navigate life using preconceived ideas, unconscious assumptions and expectations that influence what we experience.

We form this map usually in our formative years when we're creating our beliefs about who we are, what others are like by comparison, and a generalised view of what life is.

Most of us don't update these beliefs, and we live into a habitual way of being, creating a future that is drawn from our past. In this way, we don't really exercise our free will. We drift through life, creatures of habit.

REFLECTION

What do you think about life?

You could try completing this sentence: Life is…

Do you always think this way about life, or does it change depending on your mood?

HOW FIXED ARE WE REALLY?

I was taught in my psychology training that personality was fixed and consistent. Various psychological studies have attempted to measure personality: from the 'big five' to the Myers-Briggs and beyond. But what strikes me most is how personalities can actually change and transform. If we can act 'against' our personality sometimes, then is it really such a fixed thing?

What if personality tests weren't measuring a fixed personality, but instead they were mostly just measuring our habitual ways of thinking and patterns of behaviour that stem from that thinking? If this is true, then because thinking can change in a single moment, we can change too.

During a client session several years ago, I first started to question how fixed personality really was. My client, Laura, described to me that she was an introvert and liked being by herself most of the time. In the next sentence, however, Laura also described how she got nervous around people, and when I asked her why she thought this happened, said it was because she didn't think people liked her.

What follows here is my exploration with Laura into how much her preference for being by herself was actually fixed, and how much was due to her thinking.

Chris: If you didn't get nervous around people, do you think you'd enjoy hanging out with others more?

Laura: Well, people don't like me, so no.

Chris: Oh, ok, so if people did like you, do you think then that you'd enjoy socialising more?

Laura: Yes, but I don't see how that's possible.

Chris: When did you make up your mind that people don't like you?

Laura: I don't know. I guess I used to have friends.

Chris: When did that change?

Laura: I remember moving schools when I was younger, and didn't know anyone. I didn't really know how to make friends, and I remember thinking that no one liked me.

Chris: What did you do from there?

Laura: I just kept myself to myself. I used to actually be quite outgoing in my old school.

Chris: So you moved schools and didn't know anyone. And you made that mean that people didn't like you. That way of thinking hurt, and so you withdrew. Did you consider that what you believed about yourself, that people don't like you, wasn't actually true?

Laura: It felt true.

Chris: Well, we don't feel the truth, we feel our thinking. A belief is just what you made up in your head. It doesn't mean it's true. If you take a present look right now, do you think you thought this in a moment of clarity, or in a time of hurt and stress?

Laura: Definitely hurt and stress.

Chris: What happens if you look at this through the lens of clarity, rather than hurt and stress?

Laura: I was just a bit shy and didn't know anyone. People like me. My friends always say nice things about me.

Chris: So, do you think that if you believed that people liked you, you'd be more social?

Laura: Yes, like I used to be.

Chris: So, what's stopping that from being possible?

Laura: Just my thinking.

Chris: Yes. Perhaps you could be who you were before you decided this about yourself?

If you're living in a personal reality where people don't like you, it makes perfect sense to avoid people. When thought doesn't look like thought, it becomes your reality. You can be living in a world of thought, and not even know it. Laura saw through her thinking that people didn't like her and started to engage more socially. It turns out that she stopped identifying as an introvert when she was less anxious about spending time with people.

SEEING THROUGH THE WALLS

When you see your own mind-made prison for what it is, you're truly free. So what is the prison made of?

The walls of your prison are made of thought.

If you've completed the reflections, you'll get a sense of what your prison is. The walls look something like this:

I'm...
Others...
Life...

What follows after the ... is thought.

And when you can truly see on a gut level that it's thought, you're free.

REFLECTION

Now, can you go back to when you first believed these negative things about yourself, life and others? When did things actually start looking like that for you?

Can you remember a time, or an era in your life, where things felt off, wrong, stressful or painful?

Using your previous reflections above, you can now explore where some of this comes from. You might like to consider a past hurt and look at the difference between what happened and the story you created. The more you can see the distinction between the two, the more you'll see through the part that you created in your mind.

Complete the below table to help you clean up what happened versus what you made it mean:

Situation	Thought (what we add to it)
e.g. Got one question wrong	e.g. I'm stupid Life is hard Others are intelligent

Although it probably looks like both things, the situation and the thought, happened together, perhaps you can now see the separateness of them. One happened in reality and could be witnessed on camera, by a third party, as if filmed for your life's documentary. And the other was the commentator, the inner voice in your mind. The habitual narrator of your own personal experience.

Notice that it is **a** story, not **the** only possible story. And if it's a story, it's not true.

SUPERSTITIONS

Imagine that someone comes to you for help because they are exhausted. You ask them why they are so tired, and they explain how exhausting it is doing their job. It turns out that their job is to clean the pavements in town. They go up and down the streets, clearing and cleaning wherever pedestrians walk.

Whilst that does sound like it could be tiring, imagine that the level of exhaustion this person describes seems a bit out of proportion to their activity. You ask more questions, and they explain how the most exhausting thing is trying to avoid all the cracks in the pavement whilst trying to do their job.

"What do you mean by avoiding the cracks?" You ask.

"Well, you know that if you step on a crack, it's bad luck, isn't it?" They reply.

"Is it?" You say.

"Of course. If I step on a crack, then something bad will happen."

You remember that you heard that superstition when you were a kid, too, but you also know it's not true. "Do you really believe that?" You ask.

"Well, yes", they reply.

"But that's not true. I must have stepped on hundreds of cracks in my life, and I'm ok. I'm sure you could stop trying to avoid them and just get on with your job. You'd be a lot less tired if you didn't have to focus on trying to avoid all the cracks and just clean the pavement!"

"But what if something bad happens?"

"Well, it might, but not because you've stepped on a crack."

"No, I'm not willing to take the risk. Can you still help me with my exhaustion?"

When thought doesn't look like thought, it looks like reality. What do you naturally want to do for this person? Help them with their symptoms of tiredness? Or help them see that the root cause of their suffering is, in fact, their thinking?

REFLECTION

What are you believing that's true but might actually be just your thinking?

FROM SYMPTOMS TO ROOT CAUSE

Chloe came to see me because she wanted me to provide her with some tools and techniques to help her cope with people-pleasing and perfectionism. Here's what happened:

Chris: I could give you some strategies, but that would just be treating the symptom. Would you rather get to the root cause rather than just treat the symptom?

Chloe: What is people pleasing a symptom of?

Chris: Let me put it another way. Everything we do, or don't do, makes perfect sense to us on some level, whether that's conscious or unconscious. Why do you think it might make sense to you to get everything perfect and please others?

Chloe: Oh. Because I'm scared that I'm not good enough.

Chris: That then makes sense from that perspective. So, how much do you think it's true that you're not good enough, and how much do you think that's a thought?

Chloe: I think it's true.

Chris: So do you see how that's the underlying cause? If you didn't believe that you weren't good enough, would you still need to get everything perfect and please everyone else?

Chloe: I see that. So, how do we get rid of the root cause?

Chris: You have to see that it's not true that you're not good enough. Have you always thought that about yourself? Or can you remember a time when you didn't think it?

Chloe: I suppose I never used to think about it when I was younger.

Chris: So, when did you decide you weren't good enough?

Chloe: I don't know, I just remember thinking it a lot when I would get things wrong and people were upset with me.

Chris: I'm not good enough sounds like half a sentence to me. Not good enough at what?

Chloe: Hmmm, yeah, I see what you mean.

Chris: That's how we know it's a childlike way of thinking. It's how a child would think about themselves. So do you think that it's true that you're not good enough, full stop?

Chloe: I guess not. I mean, there are some things that I'm not good enough to do.

Chris: Yes, me too, but that's very different. I'm not good enough to get in the Guinness Book Of World Records for most things. Actually, probably anything! But that doesn't mean that I'm not good enough. When you decided that you weren't good enough, how old do you think you were?

Chloe: Probably about six.

Chris: Six-year-olds are great, but would you let a six-year-old run your life?

Chloe: I've never thought about it like that. No!

Chris: Well, that's what you're doing.

Chloe: Yeah, I am.

Chris: Plus, you were upset when you said this to yourself, right? Have you ever said something to someone that you didn't mean in a moment of hurt?

Chloe: Yes of course.

Chris: Would you want them to believe it for the rest of their lives, even though it wasn't true?

Chloe: Wow, no. So I don't need to believe this anymore!

Chris: That's right. So does it still make sense to you to get everything perfect and please everyone else?

Chloe: No, not at all!

It isn't always obvious to us that we create our own experience of life, so we often create less-than-ideal realities for ourselves. The good news is that as soon as we truly see that our personal realities are created with thought, these prison walls are far more malleable than they might appear.

KEY INSIGHTS

◆ We are not fixed in our personalities, and personality tests often measure habits and habitual ways of being.

◆ We create an image of ourselves, others, and life, often in times of stress and/or hurt, and we tend to keep hold of those images.

◆ We often don't see the thoughts that limit us, but we can see them in a single moment and be free from them.

FROM INSIGHT TO ACTION

If you saw through the thinking that's getting in the way of who you would love to be, what would you love to do that you're not currently doing?

CHAPTER 5

MIND-MADE PRISONS

'What we call the personality is often a jumble of genuine traits and adopted coping styles that do not reflect our true self at all but the loss of it.'
Gabor Maté

Most of our lives are spent trying to break free from these mind-made prisons that we unknowingly create for ourselves. Unfortunately, most of what we try to do to gain freedom ends up creating more limitation.

If you consider for a moment why you do most of what you do, what's the answer?

If your answer is because you choose to, then you are truly free.

But if your answer is because you think you need to, should do, or have to, then you're coming from a place of limitation, reaction and survival.

At one point in my career, I was working as a Senior Lecturer in CBT, and also served as a Senior Psychotherapist and Wellbeing Lead. Despite my success on paper, as far as I was concerned, a part of me needed to get these high positions in order to prove to myself and others that I wasn't stupid.

What was really motivating me was my insecurities, and so I was coming from a place of reactivity and anxiety, trying to escape my mind-made prison, whilst at the same time, reinforcing the very belief that I was trying to escape.

When you do what you do, are you coming from a place of freedom, or a place of reactivity, wanting simply to get through life?

As a recap, recall that who we think we are, is primarily based on a decision we made about ourselves at some point in the past, and this is what creates our self-image, or identity. This decision is usually a reaction, a survival response to something that happened that hurt.

We then come from this place of insecurity and reaction, and we either surrender to the perceived truth of it, or we try to overcompensate for it by proving that it's not true, resulting in things like perfectionism or being a workaholic.

I once had a client, Naomi, who told me she would always try to prove people wrong if they told her, or even implied, that she couldn't do something.

Naomi: When someone tells me that I can't do something, I always do it to prove I can.

Chris: What if you don't want to do it?

Naomi: I would still do it to prove them wrong.

Chris: So, if someone tells you that you can't do something that you don't want to do, you still do it? That doesn't sound very free. Why would you do that?

It turned out that Naomi had the belief of "I'm not capable" and tried to overcompensate for that by rising to any challenge, even if that challenge went against her values.

Naomi often did things in her life that she didn't want to do (running a marathon, for example, or taking a promotion she didn't want, eating raw sushi, etc.); she felt compelled to do them because she was unconsciously trying to escape the painful idea that she wasn't capable. Whilst it's the most natural thing to do in the world to try and get away from something that hurts physically, in attempting to escape the psychological belief, she was reinforcing it.

By trying to break free of the belief that "I'm not capable", she was living a life of limitation, where she wasn't free to say no to challenges. Once she began prioritising her freedom over her thinking, she found herself dismissing challenges much more easily unless she genuinely wanted to pursue them.

Building on the previous chapter, as well as developing beliefs about myself, life, and other people, I created a strategy to navigate life, which looked like this:

Situation	Thought (what we add to it)
I got a question wrong	*I'm stupid* *Others are more intelligent than me* *Life is going to be hard for me* *I need to work harder and longer than everyone else.*

What I came to see was that working harder and longer, not only became a problem in itself, but it also reinforced the very thing I was trying to escape.

'The greatest prison you will ever live inside is the prison you create inside your own mind.'
(Dr Edith Eger)

REINFORCEMENT

We habitually live from and into the beliefs that we created. When we create a reality where we feel "not good enough" or "life is hard", it makes perfect sense, given that perceived reality, to develop a series of coping mechanisms and strategies to navigate life. But on a deeper level, it doesn't make sense, because those thoughts are never true.

The problem with trying to escape a mind-made limiting belief is that by fighting it, you're treating it as if it were a real thing, thereby reinforcing the very thing you are trying to get away from. Unconsciously the very thing that we're trying to get away from, is what's driving us.

It's like explaining to a 5-year-old that monsters under the bed don't exist, versus going through a series of rituals every night to keep the monsters at bay. The potential problem with the latter is that the child will think that monsters are real, but you need to do "x-y-z" to stop them from coming to get you.

DISTORT INFORMATION TO FIT
IN WITH OUR PERSONAL
REALITY

OVERCOMPENSATE

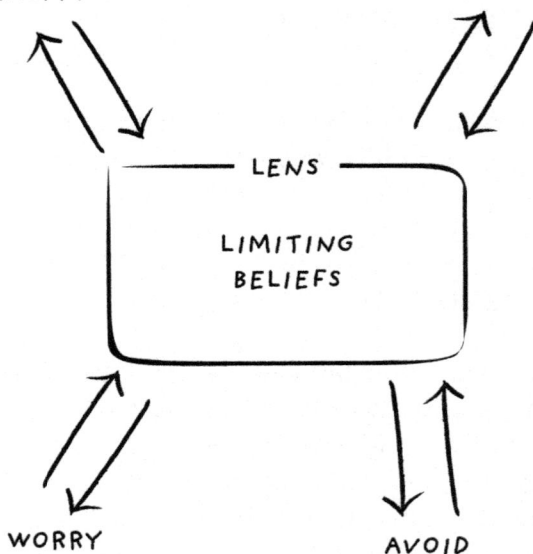

LENS

LIMITING
BELIEFS

WORRY

AVOID

Your beliefs work the same way. You needn't try to get away from them, because they aren't true, (true meaning that they don't exist outside your thinking about it).

We could, if we wanted to, go our entire lives trying to avoid being hurt like we once were, but this would leave us in a near-constant state of reaction. And we might not even know we're doing it.

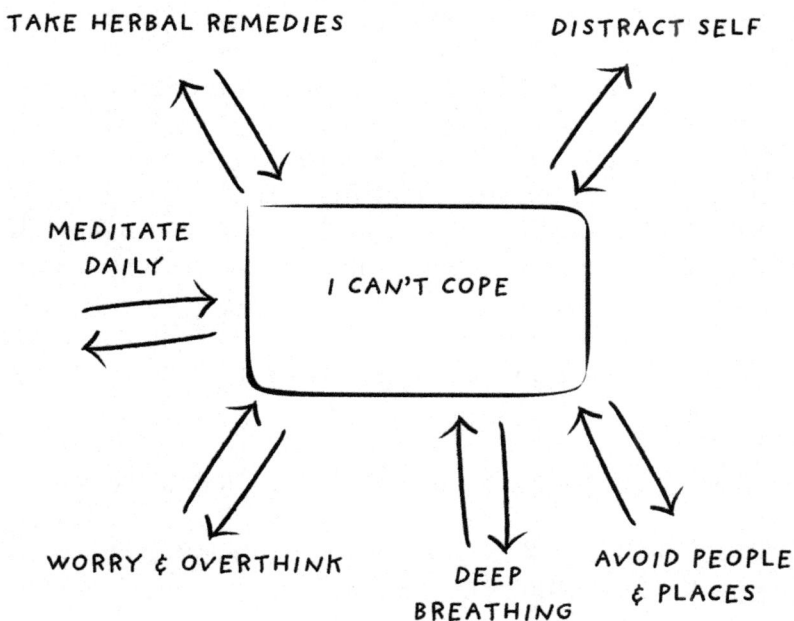

TAKE HERBAL REMEDIES   DISTRACT SELF

MEDITATE
DAILY
                    I CAN'T COPE

WORRY & OVERTHINK   DEEP   AVOID PEOPLE
                        BREATHING   & PLACES

Everything we do to escape, acts as a reinforcer, unconsciously strengthening our belief in a thought and making it appear more real to us.

You can't escape a mind-made prison from within the thinking that created it. Instead, you need to see that the walls of your prison are a thought construct.

One of my clients, Sarah, had the belief, "I can't handle anxiety". As a result, she employed a whole range of strategies and coping mechanisms to navigate the world.

She took various herbal remedies, did breathing techniques, meditation, avoided certain activities, and constantly monitored her body for any sign of anxiety.

It's really important to understand that none of these things are wrong or bad. In fact, there are many benefits to some of these things. But the problem isn't in the action itself; it's in the place you are coming from. In other words, if you have the belief of, "I can't cope" and so you employ all these coping strategies, you reinforce the very thing you are trying to escape.

When she came to see me, I asked her if any of it was helping.

Sarah: Well, not really. In fact, it's been getting worse.

Chris: Well, it will, because you're treating it as if it were true. It's like feeding fire with fire and expecting the fire to go out.

Sarah: So what do I do?

Chris: You have to see that "I can't cope" isn't really true and that it's just a thought.

Sarah: But it is true. I really can't cope.

Chris: And what if that was a lie? What if it were true that you could cope?

Sarah: Then I wouldn't need to do anything; I could just be free.

Chris: Exactly. And that's the truth. Ultimately, what you're going to come to see sooner or later if you keep looking, is that "I can't cope" is a thought, and not a truth. It's also the very core of all of your anxiety and worry. When you truly see this, you will be free.

Our personal reality acts as its own reinforcer, sustaining itself without our awareness. Even the most painful perspectives can be self-perpetuating because what you look for, you see. You end up seeing more of what maintains your reality, and you don't see things that don't fit that reality. It is entirely possible to go through life and not even notice that you're living in your own prison of thought.

'A man will be imprisoned in a room with a door that's unlocked and opens inwards as long as it does not occur to him to pull rather than push.'
(Ludwig Wittgenstein)

Imagine watching a scary movie and being scared. You don't need to do anything other than remind yourself it's not real. This is the same for your thought-created reality.

GETTING UNSTUCK

Having worked as a psychotherapist for several years, I think that the reason my work didn't get the results I might have hoped for, was because it often wouldn't get to the root of the problem and we would instead focus on the symptoms. Often the client and I would mistakenly be focusing on a consequence on a problem, not the origins. In my experience I found that most therapy is trying to manage the reactivity, not the root cause.

For example, someone might have come to see me because they wanted to learn how to cope with loneliness. But the feeling of loneliness came from not having any friends. Ultimately, they didn't have any friends because they were living in a self-imposed prison, believing that they were a social burden. Because they believed they were a burden, they failed to do what they needed to do to make and keep friends.

Why would I help someone cope with being lonely when I can help them step into a new world where they aren't a burden, and people do, in fact, want to be friends with them?

Another example of this is if somebody struggles with procrastination. Because they continually put things off, they inevitably find themselves feeling unfulfilled in life. You can either provide them with tools and techniques to help them cope with feelings of unfulfillment or you can assist them in breaking free from the procrastination.

In the world of procrastination, on some level, it makes perfect sense for them to put off things: taking the rubbish out, responding to particular emails, calling their parents, applying for a job, etc.. But when you help them see that their reason for procrastination is thought-created, it will no longer make sense to delay living their life.

Another example might be somebody who's gone to therapy because they think there is something wrong with them. They might then get a diagnosis that, unknowingly, confirms the belief that there is something wrong with them.

Similarly, if you don't feel confident in your own skin, you might try to cope with learning strategies to overcome a lack of confidence. But then you're just putting those strategies on top of the lack of confidence, reinforcing the fact that you're not confident.

When we get stuck in life, it's often because we're trying to change our lives for the better, but instead we end up acting from the very belief that's getting us stuck.

If you've been trying for some time to overcome a particular problem or struggle, this is probably why nothing you've tried has worked so far.

If you have the belief that you will only be loved if you meet others' needs before your own, then you will get into relationships from that place. You won't see possibilities outside of this reality. And if you do, it won't fit with the way you see things. In a way, it's like living in a mental cage. The escape route is there, you just can't see it.

If the root cause isn't addressed, all the tools and techniques you learn can become coping mechanisms, reinforcing the very reality you are trying to escape.

In my work, I help my clients see straight away that there is nothing wrong, other than their thinking. And even that isn't wrong. It's just limiting. This work is not really about learning something new. It's more of an unlearning, and remembering who we are before our conditioning. (We'll explore this more in chapter 6).

People very soon realise that things like people pleasing, perfectionist behaviour, overworking, and avoidance, are symptoms of believing something that's not true about themselves. As soon as they can touch their core nature, it no longer makes sense to employ coping strategies to cope with a false idea about who they are.

REFLECTION

When did you change or adapt to fit in, or get through something?

When did you get the idea that you needed to change who you are or what you do, in order to get your needs met?

TRUE FREEDOM

So, how do we really break free?

The secret is knowing that you are already free, despite any thinking that's telling you otherwise. Your true nature is inherently free, and you can do anything from this place of peace and freedom.

As I've said previously, you have to see that the walls of your prison are made of thought. You have to see through the illusion. You have to see that it's not true that you're not good enough, that life is hard, or that others are out to get you.

I know it can look real. Just like the owl looked real. But there is no owl. The owl is composed of dots, and you make it into an owl with the power of thought.

One of the most helpful things I learnt in my psychology training is that we're in one of three emotional states at any one time in life. We're either trying to get away from a perceived threat, or we're trying to get towards something that we want. When we're not in one of those motivational states, we're in a state of presence, connectedness, contentment and we are simply being.

You can't be truly free when you're habitually trying to get away from a perceived threat. If the perceived threat is made of thought, then there's nothing to escape. In the next chapter, I will be pointing you back to the place of freedom that's always inside you, no matter what.

If the perceived threat is something about yourself, then you are always going to feel some anxiety. The way our psychology works means that if you keep thinking about a perceived threat, you increase the relevance of that threat. So if you have a thought somewhere in your psychology that says "I'm not enough" or "life is hard", then unless you see through the illusionary nature of that thought, you will see it everywhere you look, and perhaps more importantly, you will feel it. We reinforce things when we perceive them as a threat.

It's well known that if you're riding a bike, you go where you're looking. Just like when my son was riding his bike last week and I shouted "watch out for the poo!" Ironically, he then focused on it and rode straight through it. My bad! If you focus on the negative, you will see the negative. Just like with riding a bike, if you focus on the obstacle, you keep coming across it. But if you focus on possibility, you see possibility.

BREAKING A HABIT OF A LIFETIME

Imagine that when you were a child, you drew a map, and on this map, you wrote down the things you thought about yourself, life, people, and circumstances.

You're now an adult, and you're still using that map to navigate life. This map represents what it's like to use your personal thinking to create your very own personal reality, your mind-made prison.

Now that you're waking up to how your psychology works, do you still want to continue to use this out-of-date map written in a child's handwriting to navigate your life?

Most of your coping mechanisms are now just habits and patterns of thinking. And it's surprisingly easy to drop a habit when it no longer makes sense to you.

Imagine if we both worked in the same office building, and every time you arrived at work, you saw me sitting at my desk with a cup of coffee, already making my way through my work. You also know that you live on the same road as me, and you know that I always leave for work after you. You ask me, "Chris, how do you get to work so quickly when you leave after me?"

I tell you which way I drive, and it turns out that you've been taking the long route to work.

Even if you've driven that way for thirty years, how long do you think it will take you to break that habit of driving that way if it no longer makes sense for you to do so?

When you see that your map of the world was made of thought, and it's no longer helpful and no longer feels good, it won't take you long to drop it and start relying more on your moment-to-moment common sense, your presence and wisdom to navigate life.

I've seen people drop habits of a lifetime in a moment. I saw a client who called themselves an alcoholic give up drinking as soon as they saw that alcohol had no inherent power over them, other than in their mind. I saw a friend settle into an incredibly intimate relationship after years of unhealthily pushing people away because they were fearful of commitment. I saw a client transform their relationship to stress when they realised they didn't have to prove themselves to anyone. It doesn't require force, effort or even willpower; it simply needs to make sense.

113

COPING STRATEGIES

When we experience something that hurts, we naturally attempt to avoid being hurt in that way again. This is usually done unconsciously, and we can form our personal reality based on these hurts. In the same way as we create a mental map of life, others and ourselves, we also create rules to live by, and we develop coping strategies to survive, based on what we've decided about that reality.

Coming from the survival mode of fight, flight, or freeze, we navigate life by the rules we've created to cope with life, people and situations given the harsh thought-created reality we find ourselves in.

Due to the fact that we're such creatures of habit, we rarely stop and question our habits, let alone our habits of thought. When somethings looked the same way to you for as long as you can remember, you don't question it.

What follows is a silly example, but I think it makes the point. I recently saw my daughter, who is 2 years old at the time of writing, brush her teeth and then walk up to the sink that she couldn't reach, look up at it, and blow a raspberry.

"That's a bit odd", I thought, and left it at that.

But the next day, she again finished brushing her teeth, and looking up at the sink, blew a raspberry towards it.

I looked at my wife and said, "What is she doing?"

"I don't know", she replied.

And then I realised. She's been watching us brush our teeth and then spit out our toothpaste in the sink. In her innocent, two-year-old mind, my wife and I were simply blowing a raspberry at the sink once we'd finished brushing.

She was copying us and had developed her own habit.

Now, at some point, I'm sure she might question this behaviour! But imagine she got to her twenties or thirties and one day her own partner, if she has one, says to her, "Why do you blow a raspberry at the sink after brushing your teeth!?"

She would have no idea!

Sometimes, we don't question our own reality, even though it doesn't make any sense. I've found in my work with clients that often they have no idea why they have some of the habits they have. They've been doing it for so long that they can't remember why it started.

For another example, let's take the following conversation I had with Tony, who came to me for help with burnout.

Tony: I'm burnt out, and I need you to help me recover so I can get back to work.

Chris: Ok, I can help with that. So, what do you think led to you burning out?

Tony: I have no idea, that's your job, I just need to get over it as quickly as possible.

Chris: Ok, but if we don't look at the root cause, you might end up back here again pretty quickly. Why are you so keen to get back to work?

Tony: I've got so much to do. I can't just sit around.

Chris: Do you always feel like you've got a lot to do?

Tony: Yes. Always. That's why I work 14 hours a day.

Chris: Wow, no wonder you are burnt out. Do you ever stop?

Tony: No, I don't have time to slow down, let alone stop.

Chris: Do you see how this way of thinking has led to you burning out, and will lead to the same again?

Tony: What way of thinking?

Chris: That you don't have time to slow down because you've always got so much to do.

Tony: That's not thinking, that's just fact.

Chris: What do you think would happen if you did slow down, and say, just worked 8 hours a day?

Tony: Things wouldn't get done, and it would be a disaster.

Chris: And what would that mean to you?

Tony: I've failed. I'm a failure.

Chris: What would things not getting done have anything to do with you being a failure?

Tony: I don't know. I've just always assumed that if I don't work hard, I'll be a failure.

Chris: Do you apply that same logic to other people?

Tony: No, I guess not.

Chris: I'm just wondering why it makes sense to you that you would be a failure if you didn't get things done, but other people wouldn't be a failure under the same circumstances?

Tony: I don't know.

Often, our coping strategies create their own problems, like with Tony burning out. Tony had developed a habit of thought where he assumed that if things didn't get done, it would mean he was a failure.

Just like my daughter blowing raspberries at the sink, Tony didn't know why he was doing what he was doing, and he hadn't really questioned it. But as Tony came to see that failing at something had nothing to do with him being a failure, it no longer made sense for him to have to burn himself out, and he was free to slow down and enjoy work and life.

If some of what you call your personality is just a series of habits you developed, and decisions you made when not getting your needs met, then you can change those habits and adaptations as soon as they no longer make sense to you.

117

Here's something I realised about the root cause of most, if not all behaviours;

Everything we do and don't do, on some level, makes perfect sense to us, given the reality that we think we're living in.

ADAPTATIONS

If you've ever had to adapt to get through something, then you'll know that sometimes these adaptations can be extremely helpful. But if they're made unconsciously, and we keep them up, the adaptations themselves can become a problem.

One of my old friends was a professional actor. When I exclaimed how cool I thought that was, he told me that he hated it.

When I asked him why he did it, he told me that it's what he needed to do to be recognised in the world. He explained that in his mind, he had to become perfect at something in order to be appreciated.

The more he explored this, the more he saw that acting wasn't an authentic desire for him, and the more he lost his taste for it. It was especially easy for him to give it up when he found that people would love and appreciate him for who he actually was, and not what he achieved.

If you had to become someone or something in order to feel loved, worthy, or whole, then that's not who you are; it's who you became. In other words, you are more than who you have adapted to be (more of this in the next chapter).

According to the National Institute of Mental Health, the thing that most people are scared of is public speaking. We are social creatures, and we fear rejection. If we learnt that in order to be loved and accepted, we need to adapt our behaviour in some way, then from that perspective, it makes perfect sense that we would strive and struggle our way to try and fit in and be liked and accepted by others. Speaking in public can often bring up the fear of being rejected.

Sometimes we can get lost in self-development, trying to become the best version of ourselves. But what if the best version of ourselves is just us? Authentic, little old us. Our natural self, minus the coping strategies we think we need.

REFLECTION

I invite you to ponder again that babies are naturally happy, free, loving, and full of life. When did this change for you?

How did you compensate for something that hurt you and what became your coping strategies to get through life?

How did you adapt in order to survive life?

If life is a game to be played, rather than something to be survived, what would you love to let go of?

The good news is that you won't ever lose anything from changing these adaptations. You won't lose your ability to do things well or to be kind to people. In fact, you'll find that your capacity and productivity will increase because you'll be less caught up in your personal thinking and more able to utilise your inner knowing, and thereby make the most of what you have available in your resources.

You also won't lose any part of yourself. Whilst we can change our adaptations, we can't change who we are at our core. You are who you are before your conditioning.

The more awake we get to who we really are, the more authentically ourselves we become.

REFLECTION

Think of some of your actions, habits and behaviours. When you do what you do, are you coming from a place of freedom, or are you coming from a place of survival or lack?

What would it be like if instead of coming from that place of insecurity, you came from a place of freedom? What might that feel for you? What might the impact be on yourself, and on those around you?

KEY INSIGHTS

◆ Much of what we might call our personality is formed based on our thinking that something was wrong. It is a survival-based adaptation, not who we truly are.

◆ We live in a mind-made prison, and the walls are created by our own limited thinking.

◆ We reinforce these thoughts with our behaviours, habits, and thinking, making them seem more real.

◆ Seeing through these thoughts gives you freedom.

◆ Breaking old patterns of behaviour is easy when they no longer make sense to you to do them.

FROM INSIGHT TO ACTION

What are you doing to try and escape a limiting belief? What action could you drop that might be reinforcing this belief?

CHAPTER 6

BEING YOU

'If it feels like there's something missing in your life. It's probably you.'
Robert Holden

When I was 13 years old, I was at school in a maths lesson, and the teacher read out an algebraic problem for the class to solve.

Then something peculiar happened.

I watched my mind solve the maths problem as if in front of my eyes, as if I could see my brain performing the calculations. It felt as if I could simply sit back and witness the event, like an impartial observer.

I realised then that there was a separateness between me and my thinking.

It was as if there were two of me. There was me, and there was everything else I could observe, including my thinking.

So far, we've been implicitly asking the question: if you are not your thinking, who are you? If I were to now ask you this question: 'Who are you?', what would you say?

The chances are that you might tell me your name, and maybe something about the roles you currently have in life, such as your occupation and marital status. You might even go a bit further and tell me about your religion, or your life circumstances, habits, and descriptions of what you do. If and when you feel safe with me, you might even tell me things that you don't like about yourself, such as believing that you're afraid of being a failure, or not good enough.

But none of that is who you are.

Who you are is deeper.

'If the voice in your head is you, then who's the one listening to it?'
(Alan Watts)

Recently, I was knocking a hole in a wall at home, and my Son asked me, "Daddy, are you a builder now?"

Although many of us identify with our roles, they're not who we are. You are not a builder, a nurse, a CEO, or a bus driver. You're not the role you carry out, because this role can change. If it can change, it is ultimately not *you*.

You are not your body.

If you accidentally chopped your finger off, you don't go thinking that you are your finger, or that your finger is you.

124

You might think, "Wait, but that's my finger", but it's not who you are. Neither are you your leg. Your torso. Your head. You are not your brain. Your body is comprised of these things, but it is not who you are.

Whilst you might identify with your body, it is *you* who is identifying with it.

You are not your conditioning.

You are not your nervous system.

You are not your moods.

You are not your thoughts.

You are not your history, your behaviours, your emotions, or what goes through your mind.

You are the observer of all of these things. The ideas you have of who you are, are just that - ideas. You are the one who has the ideas.

If there's **you**, and the **thing** that **you** can be aware of, then you can see the separateness between you and the thing that you can be aware of. Therefore, those things in your consciousness are not you. You are the one who is conscious of them.

So, who are you?

Well... you're you. But that's not Chris or Laura, Tony or Sabrina. You are not your name.

What if your parents had called you by a different name? Would that change who you are?

What if you had been switched at birth and you were raised by different parents in a different home, in a different country, with different circumstances, and therefore different conditioning and experiences? Would you still be you?

Of course you would.

Even if you had a whole raft of different experiences in life, different thoughts and influences, you would still be you.

The you that I'm pointing towards is the very essence of you. It's the you that's always been there, long before your thinking got involved, long before the ideas you had or created about yourself. It's intangible.

And this is an incredibly freeing truth to realise. When you recognise who you are on a gut level, and you live from this place, you'll have constant access to wellbeing and a state of flow.

THE ESSENCE OF YOU

Imagine that we were to now ask you the same question of 'who are you', but this time, you're not allowed to use your memory to answer the question.

If you can't use your memory, this means you can no longer recall your own face and what it looks like. Neither do you have any memories, ideas, or thoughts about who you are or who you have been prior to now.

126

Instead, you have to look inside.

Let's try it.

Who are you?

And if you can't use your memory to answer, you don't even know your name or occupation. You don't know if you are a Father, Son, Mother, or Sister.

So, who are you?

You'll soon see that you can't use thought to answer the question.

Close your eyes and go inside and see... **Who am I?**

If you look deeply enough, you'll get a felt sense of self. It might take a minute, but soon you'll find the you that's always there. That's *always* been there.

This felt sense is the very essence I'm talking about. The you that you'd be if we were to transplant your consciousness into a different body. The you that is unchangeable. You, uncontaminated by thought. As much as your face and your behaviour have changed over time, there is the you that is aware. This is the authentic you.

It's an indescribable deep sense of **being**.

Notice that this you, is the same you who observes the outside world.

Just like if I held a banana up to you, you would see the banana. You wouldn't get confused and think that you are the banana. You're just you – the observer. You can observe your thoughts independently in the same way as you observe the banana.

If you look for yourself, you'll soon see that you are not your thoughts. You are the observer of your thoughts. You are the watcher. This is who you are. The less you identify with your personal thinking, the more you identify with the awareness that is separate from it.

Your best self, your highest self, is just you. Authentic you before your thinking gets involved. Lower states of mind are simply when we've forgotten who we are, and we misidentify ourselves with thought.

Going back to the essence of yourself means that you can immediately lose all the baggage you carry around that weighs you down. And you can rest in this space at any time.

Sometimes when I'm helping someone get in touch with themselves, they point to a part of their body. It's usually in the chest or stomach area. I notice that they never point to their head.

'The feeling of your inner body is formless, limitless and unfathomable. You can always go into it more deeply.'
(Eckhart Tolle)

BEYOND SELF-IMAGE

It's very easy to lose touch with your authentic self in an idea of who you *think* you are. We all have a self-image where we create an idea of who we think we are and mistakenly think this is us, forgetting that we're actually the ones who **created** the image, and that we're not the image itself.

Imagine drawing a self-portrait, and it's such a good representation of yourself that you start to forget that it's a picture of you and not actually you. That's what we do, and we call it self-esteem or self-image.

Self-esteem is what you think of yourself, whether it's positive, negative, or anywhere in between. If you think you're confident, intelligent, or stupid, this is your idea of yourself, your image of yourself. It's not who you are. You're the one who's holding on to the image.

I used to believe that there was something wrong with me, and I would often pursue self-help tools and techniques in an attempt to fix myself. Then one day I realised one of the most helpful and freeing things I've ever realised, which is the difference between there actually being something wrong with me, and me having the *thought* that there was something wrong with me. I realised that I didn't need to fix the thought "there is something wrong with me", because it was an idea of me, and not me. If I am not my thinking, I don't need to fix my thinking.

We also have an image of how we think others see us. Often, we try extremely hard to get others to like this image, and we can end up sacrificing our own authentic self and our desires to create a positive self-image.

If you were to ask a two or 3-year-old who they are, they probably wouldn't really understand the question. They might give you their name, but they've yet to form much of an image of themselves.

At a certain point, we get an idea of who we are based on the experiences we've had, and we largely tend to keep to that idea. When we say people don't change, it's because we don't tend to update the idea of who we are, and so we live into the image we have of ourselves.

In the popular movie Forrest Gump, there's a scene where Forrest and his friend Jenny are talking about who they are going to be when they grow up. Jenny asks him, 'Forrest, who do you want to be?'

Forrest replies 'Won't I always be me?'

In this beautiful bit of dialogue, you can see there is an untouched self that's always been there for Forrest that will never change. This is his (and your) authentic, natural self.

Some of us forget who we are because we get so caught up in the noise around us in society, and in our minds. But if we simply look at what's there prior to the image we have of ourselves, we come back home.

Don't be surprised if you are brought to tears by the sheer joy of touching your inner essence; it's beautiful.

'All we are is peace, love, and wisdom, and the power to create the illusion that we are not.'
(Jack Pransky)

INNATE POSSIBILITY

We were all born perfect, whole and complete. We are free to become anything we want to become, or to be anyone we want to be. Our future is full of possibility and potential. If I were to show you a picture of a newborn baby, the chances are that you'd get a sense of this potential.

We each start off like a blank page. When I ask group participants to ponder and consider what it's like to be a baby free from too much thinking and conditioning, they come up with something like this:

FREEDOM   PURE CONSCIOUSNESS

                                    PEACE

SPIRIT   OPENNESS

                                    LIGHT
PRESENCE

                      PURE POSSIBILITY
LIMITLESS POTENTIAL

The truth is, your inherent nature never left you. You are still the same essence, at its core, free, light, and joyful.

Sadly, we often forget that our worth and value are inherent.

As time goes on, we start to get ideas about who we are. These ideas begin to happen when we realise that we are separate from our primary caregiver. I see it like this:

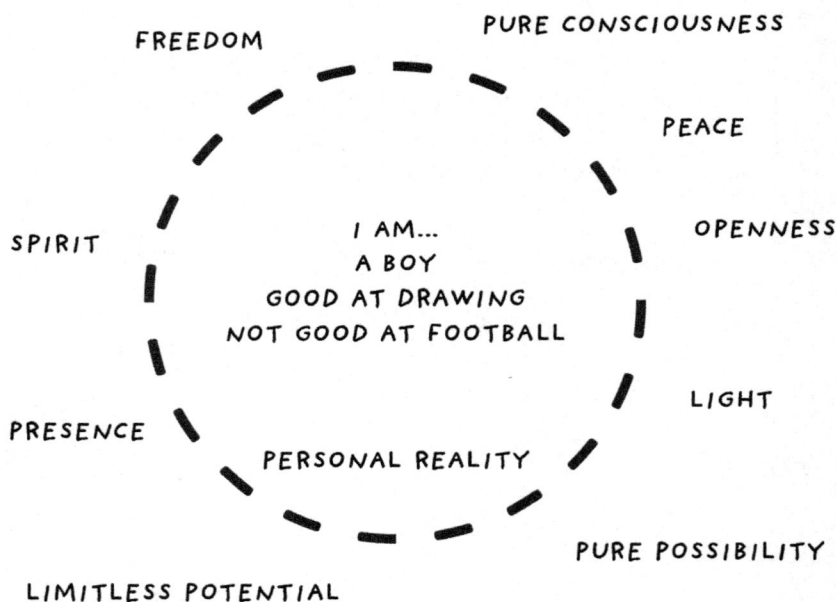

FREEDOM   PURE CONSCIOUSNESS

PEACE

SPIRIT   I AM...   OPENNESS
A BOY
GOOD AT DRAWING
NOT GOOD AT FOOTBALL

LIGHT

PRESENCE

PERSONAL REALITY

PURE POSSIBILITY

LIMITLESS POTENTIAL

Then something happens that starts to define us, and these ideas don't look like ideas to us. As I've said previously, we misidentify with them. They become solid and fixed and cloud over our natural, clear mind. Which I imagine in my mind as something like this:

FREEDOM   PURE CONSCIOUSNESS

                                    PEACE

           I AM...
SPIRIT   NOT GOOD ENOUGH   OPENNESS

                                    LIGHT
PRESENCE
           PERSONAL REALITY

                        PURE POSSIBILITY
LIMITLESS POTENTIAL

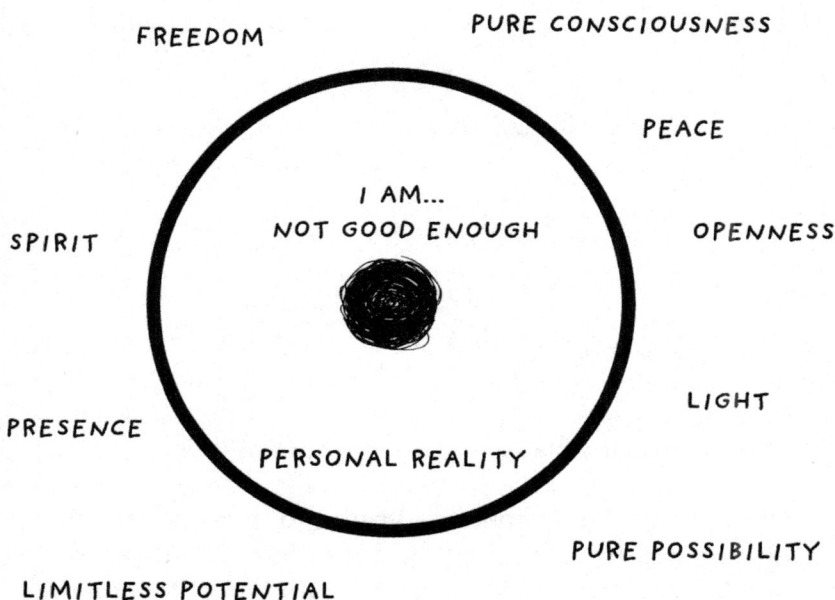

Some ideas take up more of our awareness than others and
stay stuck in our awareness. For example, a young girl or
boy might grow up thinking they have nothing interesting
to say, and this might be based on the chastisement they
experienced by a parent or caregiver at an early age, any
time they spoke. The mistake the mind of the child then
makes is to believe in this idea. The more they believe in it,
the less likely they are to open up and speak, the more likely
they are to limit themselves to silence and not making
contributions. They forget their true nature, their creative,
intelligent self underneath it all. The task, then, is to
remember this true nature.

The mistake we make is believing the lies we tell ourselves.

Finding yourself isn't learning something new; it's remembering who you are before the ideas you created.

> *'Most people live, whether physically, intellectually, or morally, in a very restricted circle of their potential being.'*
> (William James)

Our story of who we think we are gets very familiar. But just because it's familiar, doesn't mean it's true. We create our sense of self. I'm inviting you to go back to that place of creation. That blank space of pure possibility.

It's like we live in boxes. Limiting ourselves with our thinking and reinforcing that thinking with our actions and habits. We then look out from that box through the lens of our limiting beliefs.

REFLECTION

What if we're born inherently free and we lost touch with that innate freedom when we believed something about ourselves that wasn't true?

What if life were like a blank page, full of possibility? (Or like a box of chocolates, if you prefer Forrest Gump's analogy).

What if we then filled that blank page with our thinking about who we are, what was possible for us, and what life and people are like?

TWO WAYS OF BEING

Just like I could observe my brain working out a maths sum, I can observe my habitual thinking.

I then get to decide if I'm going to identify as my thinking, or the one observing my thinking. The more I identify as the observer, the more present I am, the quicker I bounce back to my wellbeing, and the more peace I feel.

You can either be identified as the essence of you, who you actually are before thought, which is a state of presence and flow. Or you can be identified as your self-image, the ideas you have of who you are. The more you see this, the more distinct the choice becomes.

These are two different states. One is on the level of pure presence and being with a clear mind. And one is on the level of thought/story.

When you are in touch with the authentic you, it has a feeling to it. Previous clients and participants of workshops have described it using the following words:

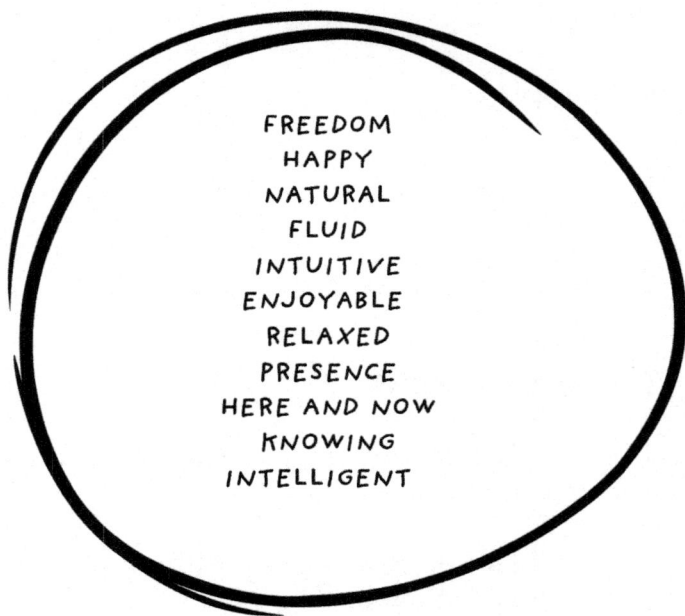

FREEDOM
HAPPY
NATURAL
FLUID
INTUITIVE
ENJOYABLE
RELAXED
PRESENCE
HERE AND NOW
KNOWING
INTELLIGENT

When we're getting stuck in life, it's usually because we're not being ourselves, and therefore, we're not acting intelligently.

The voice of wisdom that you hear is you/who you are. You are not your habitual thoughts.

A former client, Kevin, came to see me because he was struggling with his business. He was losing money and believed he had a history of making bad financial decisions. One thing that Kevin said on more than one occasion, in our first meeting, was that other people know better than he does. Kevin had an image of himself as someone who made bad decisions, generally. And so within that self-image, it made perfect sense for him not to trust himself and to look to others for advice.

Kevin and I had been exploring habitual thinking versus his inner wisdom:

Chris: Why do you think you're not being successful in business?

Kevin: I just don't think I'm cut out for it. I'm just bad at making decisions.

Chris: What makes you think that?

Kevin: Just past experiences.

Chris: What if it's not true that you're bad at making decisions, and it's just an idea you've picked up about yourself from some things that haven't gone your way?

Kevin: That would be nice, but I don't believe that. Others seem to find it so much easier than I do to make good decisions.

Chris: What if you did believe that you could make good decisions?

Kevin: It would be so freeing. I could just let go of my overthinking and trust myself.

Chris: So why don't you believe that you can just let go of your habitual thinking and make whatever decision seems most intelligent to you now, in the moment?

Kevin: I just remember when I made a bad business decision last year, and it really cost me. Overthinking keeps me out of trouble.

Chris: I'm just wondering if, at any point when making that bad decision, your intuition told you something was off?

Kevin: Yes, but I didn't listen to it. I thought I should go with it because someone else told me to.

Chris: So what if it's your overthinking and self-doubt that got you into trouble?

Kevin: What do you mean?

Chris: Well, it seems to me that your inner wisdom knew it was a bad decision, but instead of listening to it, you listened to your habitual thinking and did what someone else suggested.

Kevin: Oh yeah! It was my overthinking that got me into the mess. My gut would have kept me out of it.

Chris: Exactly. I'd say that whenever we make unhelpful decisions for ourselves, it's because we act according to our habitual thinking, and not according to our inner wisdom. I think you ignored your inner wisdom because you made the assumption that other people know better than you.

Kevin: Yes, I can see that now. My gut would have kept me safe.

STATES BECOME TRAITS

When you see yourself as a fluid being, and not as a fixed person, it leaves you more open to transforming how you show up in life. We are, after all, a verb, not a noun. We are more like a process, a dynamic living being in flux, rather than a fixed, static thing incapable of change.

Another way of thinking about this is that we are always in a state of being. Yet we have the ability to hold thoughts and images in mind. Living into those ideas, we create what we might call a trait.

When we label ourselves as something: stupid, anxious, bad at football, incapable of finding new friends, etc., we put ourselves in a box, and we lose any chance we had of transforming. We might then dismiss opportunities we have for growth.

When we think of ourselves as some fixed thing, we *are* fixed. When we see our true nature, we are free. We are then more adaptable and creative, more able to let go, and more prone to taking action, resulting in higher performance in whichever direction we tend to point ourselves.

If I have an idea that I'm an unintelligent person not capable of much in life, it's not going to occur to me to go for big goals and achievements. If I think I'm a strong, confident and capable person, I'm naturally going to both create and look for opportunities.

If I'm in a state of being where all I see is scarcity and limitation, and I live into that, I fix that state of being, and it can become a trait. It can be something I refer to as "this is who I am, this is just my personality."

Your identity is not fixed. It consists of a bunch of ideas that you made up about yourself. If you focused less on what you thought about yourself and more on who you are at your core, you would be free to play whatever game of life you wanted to play.

Consider the following words from Michael Neill:

There is a space inside us where we are already perfect, whole, and complete. The moment we touch that space, it is as if we have come home to ourselves, no matter how long we have been away. When we rest in the feeling of this space, the feeling of it heals our minds and bodies.

When we operate from the infinite creative potential of this space, we produce high levels of performance, flow, and creative expression.

When we sit in the openness of this space with others, we experience a level of connection and intimacy that can be disconcerting until we relax into it, and it is breathtakingly enjoyable and loving once we do.

And when we explore this space more deeply, we find ourselves growing closer and closer to the divine, even if we're not sure there is such a thing and wouldn't know how to talk about it if there were.

It's possible to live in this space all the time. There is never a need to leave.

The truth is, you can't be in that deepest part of yourself and be worrying about your life. You can't be connected to the deepest space within you and still feel stressed about the way things are going.

'If you drop your ego (your image of self-importance) and simply be you—just you, whoever you are—you'll find the secret to heaven here on earth.'
(Sydney Banks)

There are no limits to the depth of this space. There are no limits to how much peace, joy, and bliss you can experience.

What's more, when you're in this space, you don't see problems anymore; you see opportunities. You don't see separation; you see connection.

When you're in this space, you feel like you want to feel all the time, and you're free to follow your heart and to be at your best. Ask yourself: What if your only job in life was to be you?

KEY INSIGHTS:

◆ You are not your roles, you are not your thinking, and you are not your body.
◆ You are an unchangeable, deep sense of being.
◆ You can go back to the essence of you without all the baggage you carry around at any time.

FROM INSIGHT TO ACTION

What behaviours would you drop if you truly saw for yourself that you were enough just being you, that you didn't need to do anything or prove anything?

To access an audio that accompanies this chapter, scan the QR code below, or visit https://chris-finn.com/beingyou

CHAPTER 7

WE FEEL OUR THINKING

'If the only thing people learned was not to be afraid of their experience, that alone would change the world.'
Sydney Banks

The other day, my son asked for a bagel. My wife toasted it to perfection, cut it in half, and took it over to him. Then, unexpectedly, he cried out and threw himself on the floor, screaming that he didn't want it cut up. I wasn't worried about him, of course, as I knew his experience would pass quickly, and that he'd be back to his natural, cheerful self, being the three-year-old that he is.

Later that day, I received an email and found myself quite upset by what I thought was a very harsh criticism. I was struck when I realised that just like a bagel can't upset my son, an email can't, in fact, bother me. I was upsetting myself with the thought of what this email meant.

What's more, I knew that I probably wouldn't still be upset in a few days' time, because I would likely have stopped thinking about it and moved on to something else. I then realised that if I wanted to, I could actively choose to stop thinking about it right now. So I did. The emotions passed mere moments later, and I was left with the clarity of mind I needed to deal with the criticism effectively.

'No one can make you feel inferior without your consent.'
(Eleanor Roosevelt)

When we know that our emotions aren't coming from bagels or emails, our experience passes just as quickly as we allow it to.

I invite you to ask yourself: Have you ever gotten upset, and then some time passes, and later you wonder what all the fuss was about? Perhaps there was a problem, and in a few days, you've completely forgotten about it? Or at least it's turned out better, or less severe, than you thought it was going to?

When you realise for yourself that the source of any upset isn't inherent in the circumstance, but in what we're adding to it with our thinking, you'll find that you will bounce back to your innate wellbeing quicker and quicker without any effort involved.

Our emotions are always completely understandable given what we're thinking, but it is also true that 100% of our emotions originate from within us, and not from outside.

WHERE IS OUR EXPERIENCE COMING FROM?

Our happiness, peace and wellbeing don't come from, say, the room we're in, the people we're talking to, the state of the weather, or the book we're reading; these emotions or states are already there on the inside, waiting for us to drop our thinking and tap into the vast reservoir of good feelings that is always and already there.

Anytime we're experiencing feelings of stress, low mood, or anxiety, it's because we're creating our own experience of those thoughts and emotions. Since we are the ones creating them, we can let them go the instant we see them for what they are and return to our natural state of peace.

The more we see how our psychology works, the more peace and joy we experience. It's not that you need "x" to be happy, it's that you **think** that you need "x" to be happy, which means you're in fact neglecting to look in the one place that happiness is… inside.

When you take away the thought that you need something outside yourself to be happy, you'll see that you're made of wellness right now in this moment, regardless of circumstances.

I think of it like playing on a fruit machine. If you attribute your happiness to winning, or anything else outside of yourself, and you say things like, "I'll be happy when…" sometimes you will win, and the thing that you're basing your happiness on will occur. But often, you'll lose. When you put your attention on rediscovering the feelings of happiness that are always already there, you win every time.

REFLECTION

Complete the following sentence with as few or as many things as you like:

I'll be happy, peaceful, and fulfilled when...

How does that feel?

What happens if you change the sentence to:

I'll be happy/peaceful/fulfilled when I stop thinking about the above...

Because we experience our thinking and not life itself, when we drop the thoughts of what external circumstances will make us happy, we stop pushing our happiness and peace away, and we access them now. Because we're then more present to life, we have a greater chance of creating what we want in life, and we'll be less hung up on the road to getting it.

At a certain stage in my life, I assumed that once I owned my own home, earned a sufficient income, and met the right partner, I would finally be happy. What I see now is that my feelings of wellbeing, happiness, and peace don't come from the outside. We have a deep reservoir of wellbeing within us at all times, which is present whenever we become quiet enough to feel it. Even when it doesn't appear to be there, it is there, but hidden by the thought-cloud of "I need a partner! I need a house! I need more money! Or I won't be happy!"

The following conversation with Peter delves deeper into emotions and their origins.

Peter: I want to grow my business, but I'm just feeling off whenever I think about expanding.

Chris: Why do you think that is?

Peter: Well, I just think it's not right for me to do any marketing or networking, which is what I'll need to do if I do want to grow, but like I say, that just doesn't feel right to me.

Chris: Where do you think this feeling "off and not right" is coming from?

Peter: It's whenever I think of advertising my services, so I guess that it's not right for me.

Chris: Well, the other day I was driving to a particular place to deliver some training, and as I arrived, I happened to look up at the logo for the company, and immediately had a bad feeling. How do you explain that?

Peter: That's your feelings telling you that something's not right.

Chris: I see it quite differently. Given that my feelings come from my thinking, rather than company logos, I did wonder why I was feeling bad, but I didn't pay it too much attention. Later, when I was pulling out of the car park, I remembered that some years ago, I had driven into this same place and nearly crashed into someone else's car, and that was where my feelings were coming from. So much of our thinking is beneath our conscious awareness, we often don't even know what we are thinking. So what do you see in this for yourself?

Peter: So you're saying the feeling "off" is coming from my thinking?

Chris: Unless you know of another mechanism that I haven't come across, which explains how a simple logo can make you feel something so strongly, then... yes.

Peter: Hmm, okay, so how can I apply this to myself?

Chris: Well, what must you be thinking about networking and reaching out to people?

Peter: They will think I'm some sleazy salesman.

Chris: So you are feeling the feelings that are coming from thinking that people will see you as a sleazy salesman. So do you see that this notion is something that you're just imagining? That nobody else but you has used the word "sleazy salesman"?

Peter: I do, yeah. Honestly, it makes a lot of sense!

There is no physical, or biological mechanism whereby a situation can make you feel a certain way. If you can see that the source of the feeling is in the way you're looking, and not inherent in the circumstance, then you're closer to a whole new experience of life.

If Peter could see that the source of his feelings was simply in the way he was looking at himself (that he himself was assuming people would see him as "sleazy"), he would be one step closer to being free to speak about his services.

The funny thing is with feelings is that your body reacts the same way to something real happening, as it does to something that you imagine happening.

If you picture something bad happening, you can really be in it and lose yourself in the daydream. Your body will react as if it is indeed happening now.

To borrow my client's phrase, I can recall a particular day when I noticed my wife was a bit "off" with me. I couldn't remember doing anything to upset her, so I asked her what was wrong. 'I had a dream that you cheated on me, ' she said.

'Is that why you've been a bit upset today?' I asked.

'Yes', she said.

'But I didn't, ' I said, defending myself.

'I know, but it still feels like you did, and I can't shake the feeling. '

After a while she did shake the feeling, but for a while, it felt real to her. Just like it feels real when we're upset, and when it later passes, we wonder why we ever got so caught up.

It's the same if you imagine your favourite food.

If you picture it, really imagine it right here in front of you, you see the colours, the texture, and even sense the smell. Then your first bite, and you'll most likely already be salivating. But where is the food? It's there, in your imagination.

Once we wake up from the daydream, we see that our experience was coming from within us, via thought. Not only do we perceive our experience, we create it.

Instead of having to manage or cope with our emotions, we can use our feelings as a guide as to whether we're using our thinking effectively or not. We are then more in touch with our natural intelligence and desires, which allows us more time, attention, and energy to create a life that we love.

Although we can't use the strength of our feelings as a guide to truth, we can always afford to trust our inner knowing. (More on this in chapter 11).

Knowing that our feelings originate from within us does not mean we resign ourselves to our circumstances. In fact, it provides us with greater clarity, intelligence, and freedom to act. I used to spend a lot of time in my head worrying about my future and problem solving possible scenarios that may or may not happen. Until, I realised that thought-created problems don't need solving because they are made up.

WHEN WE DON'T KNOW WHAT WE'RE THINKING

Sometimes we don't know what we're thinking, or even that we're thinking, but we can feel it. When you don't see what you're thinking, your feelings will tell you.

We're often not conscious of what thoughts are swimming around in our mind. But our feelings will always alert us to how we're using our thinking. If we're feeling uncomfortable, to know in the moment the source of your discomfort is in thought, and not inherent in the situation, is the answer to finding freedom from struggling with emotions and situations.

Just as you might reverse your car into a post because it was in your blind spot, hidden from view, most of our thinking is also hidden from our current level of awareness. Although it may be obvious once you see it, it's easy to miss.

There's much more going on in your thinking than you can see. We refer to these blind spots as the unconscious. The unconscious isn't some deep mystical thing. It's certainly not something to be scared of. It's just what happens to be out of your awareness at present. Just like you can't be aware of everything going on in your immediate environment simultaneously, you can't possibly be aware of everything you think at the same time. We can make the unconscious conscious at any moment if we simply look.

I often found that when applying CBT techniques to clients, they wouldn't know what they were thinking. They would know they were feeling bad, but they often couldn't find the thought that was creating the feeling. "What's going through your mind?" I would ask, but their response was frequently "I don't know".

I wish I could have seen then what I see now.

You can tell what you're thinking by the feeling.

If you're feeling stressed, you're thinking stressful thoughts. If you're feeling angry, you're thinking angry thoughts, and if you're feeling depressed, you're having depressing thoughts.

Much of our thinking, which exists outside our conscious awareness, is in the form of expectations and assumptions. It's possible that we're assuming something is wrong with us or a situation, and then we're feeling the thought that accompanies that assumption. Or it might be that we're expecting things not to go our way, or we're expecting we won't be okay at some point in the future. In that case, we're feeling the thinking behind those expectations.

It can be like we're looking out through a filter that you don't know you're looking through. We may have the unconscious assumption that "people are uncaring", and we will experience people as uncaring because we are looking through that filter.

A helpful question to ask yourself is;

How are things looking to me right now, in this very moment?

If they seem hopeful and exciting, that tells you something about what you're thinking. If things are looking bleak and scary, that also reveals something about your thought process.

Once you know what you're thinking, as long as you see its true nature is inherently illusionary and made of thought, then it tends not to be a problem. If it still looks like a problem, then you haven't really seen that it's made of thought. In fact, a good indicator that someone doesn't really see it's true thought-created nature is when they say "I know it's thought, but..." They don't actually know that it's their thinking.

REFLECTION

When was the last time you experienced some level of anxiety or worry?

Was the anxiety inherent in the situation, or was it in the way you were looking at it? What was it you were thinking, assuming or expecting?

FEELINGS AS AN ALARM

You can think of your feelings as a guide to tell you how you're using your thinking. Just as a smoke alarm in your home goes off to warn you of a possible fire, in the very same way, your painful feelings alert you to the painful thoughts you're having.

It's two very different things between believing that you need to cope with feelings that are coming from outside us, and instead, realising that your feelings are just there to tell you what you're thinking. You don't need tools and strategies to manage feelings when you see they are simply an indicator as what happens to be going through your mind at the time.

The thing is, some of us can become so habituated to feeling anxious or low that we barely notice the alarm going off. I used to live in a house where the neighbour's house alarm would often go off. It went off so often, I usually tuned out the noise. Once, when I had been in all day, my housemate arrived home and asked how long their alarm had been going off. As soon as he asked, I could hear it and realised it had been going off for hours.

In contrast to this, the more you spend time feeling good, the easier it is to notice the alarm of any hurtful feelings going off.

This is how our natural resilience works. If something is painful or unhelpful, you'll know to let go of it, in the same way your physiological system tells your hand to draw back from a hot flame.

It's the most natural thing in the world to let go of something that hurts. Whether that's physical or psychological. When we work in harmony with how the system works, we experience more peace, ease, and flow.

But we habitually don't let go. We keep thinking things that hurt. Because we have free will, we can override the natural response of letting go if we believe it will be beneficial not to let go. We can become so unconsciously and habitually conditioned to dwell on our negative thoughts and feelings because of the meaning we attribute to them.

What follows is a conversation with Sophie who was worried about having a panic attack and had years of therapy for "panic disorder", which hadn't provided any relief for her.

We'd just got to talking about her fearful thoughts of having another panic attack and her passing out from it.

Chris: So it sounds like you know already that the panic is coming from your thinking. What's stopping you from dropping these thoughts?

Sophie: I just don't know how to stop thinking them.

Chris: Well, how do you stop thinking about other thoughts that pass through your mind?

Sophie: I just do.

Chris: Exactly. There's no technique to it. You just let them go.

Sophie: But I can't just let go of these thoughts of passing out.

Chris: Why not?

Sophie: Well, they're important.

Chris: So if you don't think a thought is important, you just let it go. I'm just saying you can do the same with these thoughts.

Sophie: So, how do I not think about it?

Chris: I don't think it works like that. You can't help what pops into your mind, but if a thought pops in that you don't like, you don't have to keep thinking it. Some thoughts that pop into my mind feel horrible, and I don't want to keep them alive by going over them. It's the most natural thing in the world to stop doing something that hurts.

Sophie: I guess I've not been letting it go because I've been trying to work it out.

Chris: I can't see that there is anything to work out. We feel our thinking, and you're feeling the thinking of "I'll pass

156

out and look ridiculous". That's a scary thought. If I were to think that, I'd feel anxious too. But it's an experience created by thought.

Sophie: But what if I do pass out?

Chris: You're doing it again.

Sophie: Oh yeah!

Chris: You don't need to work any of that out. There is no problem to be solved here. You're just feeling your thinking. If you were to think that anything scary was happening, you'd feel that too. It doesn't mean anything.

Sophie: So this isn't a problem?

Chris: There's a difference between a thought-created problem and a real problem. You think that this is a problem, which is what's creating the anxiety. When you watch a scary movie on TV, you probably don't get too bothered because you know it's not real. You thinking about having a panic attack in the future isn't real. It's imagination. I know that thinking you're going to have a panic attack is much more likely to create a panic attack than not thinking it.

Sophie: Yes.

Chris: Anxiety isn't a problem to be solved. Anxiety is a feeling that comes from thinking scary thoughts. The reason none of the tools and techniques you've tried have worked for you is that you've been living in a thought-created experience where there's something wrong with your feelings, when that's just not true.

157

Sophie: So I'm feeling the feelings from thinking that there's something wrong?

Chris: Yes. If you take away that thought, what happens?

Sophie: I'm free.

Sophie was living in an experience where she couldn't let go of her anxious thoughts because she thought they were a problem to be fixed. But you can't fix a thought. Feelings are just feelings that come from thoughts, so they too are nothing to be fixed. The only problem Sophie had was believing that there was something wrong with her thinking and feelings, and that in itself is a scary thought.

THE MEANING WE ADD TO FEELINGS

Many of us have developed many unhelpful thought patterns that interfere with how our psychological system naturally functions. If I start thinking something unhelpful, I immediately notice. If I choose to, I have the free will to let my thoughts go. But if I've developed the belief that I need to keep thinking it, that it's in some way helpful to keep thinking it, it won't make sense for me to let it go because I think it's necessary to keep holding it in mind.

A feeling for some people can be a trigger for thinking that there is something wrong. It's very common to believe that not feeling happy means there's a problem. If we think this, then we can then habitually focus on the negative feeling. Or we might try to find an external cause for it, whilst looking out at life through the lens of 'there's something wrong'. This is why feelings, and emotional states can linger, instead of just passing by naturally if we let them.

If we go back to what's natural, children experience a wide range of emotions, but they pass very quickly. I've found that the only thing that keeps emotions alive in us grown-ups is that we give them credence and add meaning to them. Again, we do this innocently and unconsciously.

One of my clients, Jill, would often feel anxious, for example. Not a problem, seeing as anxiety is part of life and comes from anxious thinking. But Jill thought that feeling anxious was the worst feeling in the world. She assumed that feeling anxious meant she was "broken". Jill stopped going to the pub with friends, and even to certain friends' houses, in case she felt uneasy.

If we make the experience of anxiety mean that there's something wrong with us, the thought of there being something wrong creates more anxiety. It's a self-perpetuating cycle where we develop anxiety about anxiety.

We can sometimes make the mistake of making our feelings mean something other than us feeling whatever we're thinking. For example, it's quite common to feel anxious and then make that feeling mean that something bad is going to happen. When in actual fact, it just means that we're feeling our thinking of something bad happening.

When we mistakenly believe that our emotions mean something other than what we're thinking in the moment, we struggle. We spend time analysing our feelings and thinking there's some important and urgent information there for us to discover, when in truth, we're just feeling our thoughts.

WHAT IF FEELINGS WEREN'T PROBLEMS?

As a trained psychotherapist, I used to think that anxiety and other emotions were problems to be solved. Now I see that feelings are simply an indicator of how you are using your thinking.

One of my clients, Anna asked me recently, "I'm feeling stressed. What am I doing wrong?"

Chris: What if you're not doing anything wrong?

Anna: What do you mean?

Chris: What has feeling stressed got to do with you doing anything wrong?

Anna: Well, I must be doing something wrong; otherwise I wouldn't be feeling stressed. I've got a huge presentation coming up at work, all the building work at my house, and now my boss wants me to bring a deadline on a project forward.

Chris: That does sound like a lot! But I know enough to know that stress doesn't come from circumstance, it comes from our thinking. So what if the stress is a feeling that is telling you that you're overthinking, and you need to slow down?

Anna: But I've got too much to do to slow down.

Chris: Of course you think that you've got too much to do to slow down. That's why you're experiencing stress.

Anna: But I do have too much to do.

Chris: It might be difficult to see, but that is only one way of looking at things. Once you see that it's not the busyness or the situation causing stress, but the thought that you're doing something wrong, and that you've got too much to do, then I think you'll see clearly what you can do, and what you can't do. Do you ever have the same amount of things to do and feel on top of it all?

Anna: Yes, I do actually.

Chris: So the variable is in how you're using your thinking in the present moment, not in the bags you've got to pack and the passport you have to organise, and the meeting you've got to have with your boss to arrange the holiday.

Anna: Okay, I can see that. So maybe I just need to let go of the thought that I have too much to do. That does feel better.

Chris: And then you'll get done what you can get done, and you won't get done what you can't get done.

Anna: Yes, and I also see now that realistically I can't possibly get all that done! Part of my stress was coming from thinking that I could! But I just need to speak to my boss and tell him how much I have on.

When Anna did speak to her manager, they took some work off her as they agreed that it was too much to do. As Anna realised, her stress was also coming from the fact that she thought she should be able to do it all.

If we can get out of the way with our thinking, our wellbeing rises. We work so much better in life when we're present and engaged with what's right in front of us, rather than being lost in our thinking. However, when something doesn't go the way we think it should, we often believe there's something wrong with us, or wrong with life.

KEEPING ANXIETY SIMPLE

From what I've learnt, I would say that all problems with anxiety are due to a misunderstanding of exactly what anxiety is.

'Nothing in life is to be feared, it is only to be understood.'
(Marie Curie)

Anxiety is a moment-to-moment experience of thought and feeling.

Before my career in psychology, I once met someone who told me that they had a fear of being buried alive. At the time, I recall telling them that I had never even considered it. What was the most interesting to me, was that the more this man told me about his fear of being buried alive, the more anxious I started feeling. I recall thinking, "Why am I feeling anxious? Maybe I have a fear of being buried alive, too!"

Then I realised what was happening. I was imagining what it would be like if I were buried alive. It was terrifying. And then I realised the secret to why I didn't have a fear of being buried alive, and he did. I had never considered it until now. And he thought about it all the time. When I did think about it, of course, I felt anxious, because it's a scary thought. I intuitively asked him, "If you stop thinking about it, does it still bother you?"

"Of course it does". He replied.

"How?" I innocently and curiously asked.

He pondered for a moment. And then looked at me and laughed. "Maybe I just need to stop thinking about it".

When we mistakenly believe that anxiety is anything more than feeling our anxious thinking in the moment, we tend to develop anxiety about getting anxious. We then create a whole bunch of coping strategies and avoidance behaviours to try to avoid a feeling. We can make anxiety as complicated as we like, and I know I used to. But the simplicity is that anxiety is a feeling, and we feel our thinking.

WORRY V FEAR

Sometimes we confuse worry with fear. I think of fear as having a present moment awareness of a real threat.

This fear response is an evolutionary mechanism designed to deal with danger in real-time. It's not intended to be used for planning job interviews or first dates. Yet that's what a lot of people rely on to prepare; thinking of all the worst-case scenarios and planning for every eventuality. But that's what I call worry.

Often, when I begin to teach the difference between worry and fear in a group, before I get too far, someone will argue, "But anxiety keeps us safe".

To which I point out, "No, intelligence and wisdom keep you safe".

We don't need to experience a feeling of anxiety to not jump off a roof, or to not walk in front of an oncoming car. We have the intelligence to be aware of present-moment danger, quite naturally.

Worry is imagining something bad happening and feeling the associated feelings as if it were happening now. That's what the experience of worry is. It hurts and feels unpleasant.

Some of us are in the habit of picturing terrible things happening when we need to make a decision. Then, because we're feeling the anxiety from the image of something bad happening, we feel too scared to take any particular action.

'I am an old man and have known a great many troubles,
but most of them have never happened.'
(Mark Twain)

This is a short excerpt from a conversation I had with a client who was struggling to make a decision about whether to take a new job offer or not:

Tina: I'm just so scared of making a wrong decision.

Chris: Would you be willing to let the worry of making a wrong decision go?

Tina: But how?

Chris: That's not what I asked. Would you be willing to stop thinking about making a wrong decision?

Tina: Yes.

Chris: Ok, great. So let's explore this for a moment. Because come to think of it, I don't actually know what a wrong decision is. How would you teach me to worry about making a wrong decision?

Tina: What do you mean?

Chris: Well, I don't have the same concerns as you when making decisions. So, if I were to ask you to try and train me, or say a young child, to worry about making a wrong decision, how would you do it?

Tina: Oh, well, I'd tell them to picture all the worst things that could happen, and then try to solve each one in their mind.

Chris: Sounds fun! And what does picturing things going wrong have to do with making a decision?

Tina: Well, that's how I do it.

Chris: No wonder you're feeling paralysed with decision making. Do you realise that you're literally just picturing things happening that you don't want to happen, and then feeling the feelings of that right now as if it is already happening?

Tina: Yes, I am, aren't I?

Chris: Yes, that's why it feels so bad. The way I see it is that if something bad does happen, why can't you just deal with it at the time, if and when it does happen?

Tina: That makes sense.

Chris: Sense is good. So, from this place, can you see any reason to keep worrying?

Tina: No, I can't. I'm sure I will worry at times because it's a habit, but I don't see any reason why I can't just drop it when I notice it.

I remember being at my desk once, lost in thought, worrying about something, when my wife called me in for dinner. I sat with the kids and smiled at seeing them, when I remembered that I had been worrying just a moment ago. "What was I worrying about!? I can't actually remember!"

I tried hard to recall what I had been so worried about, when I then caught what I was doing. I was present with my kids, enjoying their company. Why was I then using the power of thought to try to create anxiety and worry? I let it go and enjoyed their company over dinner.

I often find that usually the only resistance people have to dropping worry is the idea that worry is helpful. If you believe that worry is useful, then why would you stop? I've found that as long as it makes sense for you to worry, then you will experience worry.

But worry isn't helpful. Worry is using your imagination to think of things that you don't want to happen. And it doesn't feel good. When you see this for yourself, the next time you find yourself caught in the habit of worry, you'll know by the feeling, and you can drop it in an instant because it won't make sense to you to carry on.

One of the most beautiful things that I've personally learnt from this understanding is that we can tell by the feeling if we're thinking something that's not true.

Whenever we're feeling anxious, low, stressed, or any other way we don't want to be feeling, it's because we're thinking something that's not true. Our feelings are a simple, yet profound indicator of how we're using the gift of thought.

KEY INSIGHTS:

- ◆ It hurts to think hurtful thoughts. That hurt that we feel is designed to tell us to stop thinking it. It's an alarm going off with the message: "STOP. You're thinking something that hurts".
- ◆ We all have blind spots. But your feelings will tell you how you're using your thinking.
- ◆ You are the creator of all of your feelings, including the ones that are entirely understandable and justifiable.
- ◆ We often attach a lot of meaning to our feelings, which can keep us stuck in them.
- ◆ When you're less focused on trying to solve your emotions, you have more clarity and access to your natural wisdom to deal with anything you need to deal with.

◆ Thought-created problems don't need solving because they are made up.

FROM INSIGHT TO ACTION

Now that you know that you don't need to fear feeling a certain way, what would you love to do that you've not been doing?

CHAPTER 8

THE LADDER OF MOODS

'The real voyage of discovery consists not in seeking new landscapes, but in having new eyes.'
Marcel Proust

Have you ever noticed that things look different to you depending on how you're feeling at the time?

I'm sure you have.

Try to remember the last time you spoke to a friend who has gone through a breakup: they're telling you that they'll never find anyone again, that it's all over, love, life... everything! And yet you know they'll be okay in time. "There are plenty more fish in the sea", you say. You know they're in a temporary state of low mood, not seeing things clearly.

You also know that they just need to wait until they reach a higher state of mind, and things will look entirely different to them. What appears to be a real-life problem to them, looks like a temporary state of mind to you.

We all have moods, and our moods paint the picture of life we have in the present moment. Because our moods are constantly changing, we continually experience a different life.

LOOKING THROUGH OUR MOODS

We each experience fluctuations in our moods from moment to moment, shaping our life experience from the inside out through our thoughts.

Have you ever had a problem that you just couldn't see a way out of, only to come back to it later and either the solution became apparent to you, or the problem simply seemed to disappear? This is what I call the "inner ladder" at play.

When you realise how much this ladder influences your moment-to-moment experience of life, you'll learn when to pay attention to your inner experience, and when to just let it go.

Once, when I was touring a city on a summer's day, my wife Emma and I walked into a church. I was surprised at how dark it was in there. I couldn't understand why they made it so hard to see everything.

"It's so dark in here!" I exclaimed.

She turned to me and laughed. "What?" I asked.

"You've got your sunglasses on!" She said.

Once I realised I was looking through a darkened lens, my whole experience changed. I knew I wasn't seeing things as they were.

The insight I gained is that when you know you're looking through a lens, you know that your experience will be coloured by that lens. It doesn't necessarily change what you're feeling, but it does change your experience, because you know it's not real. You also know it will change at any moment.

The inner ladder is a bit like putting on a pair of glasses with various lenses. When you're towards the top of the ladder, you have a transparent lens and a clear mind. You feel the way you want to feel all the time. You have an abundance of wellbeing, clarity, contentment, peace, inspiration and creativity. You are your highest self, and it seems that there's nothing you can't handle. There is a sense of ease, peace and contentment. You feel as free as a bird, and you naturally find yourself engaging in habits and behaviours that match this internal state. You're less focused on where to get to, because it seems like you've got everything you always wanted, and you see a vast open landscape of opportunities everywhere you look.

You also have your lower states, where you're wearing a darker lens. You experience a low mood, anxiety, and the world looks very different. You're in a subtle survival state of fight, flight, freeze, and there is no room for creativity or possibility. When we're in a low mood and have more negative, or darker, thoughts, these thoughts look and seem like the real landscape ahead of us.

We view life, people, and circumstances from our current perspective on this ladder. When we're at the top, people tend to look friendlier and more welcoming, and we create and maintain connections more easily. When we're at the bottom, people appear more threatening, and it's much harder to connect.

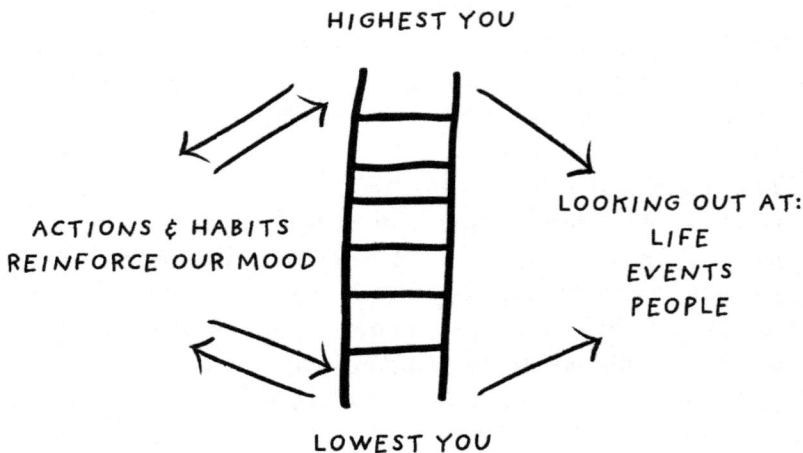

I recall a moment from my psychotherapy training when the trainer shared an example of how his wife often appeared more beautiful to him when he was in a high mood. And when he was in a low mood, she somehow looked meaner to him. It wasn't her face that had changed, it was his mood.

There's a psychological term we call "acclimatisation". We become habituated to things that which we're repeatedly exposed to. There is also an often used metaphor to explain this concept, involving a frog and boiling water. *Please don't try this at home because… It's not true! Nevertheless, the metaphor goes like this;

If you put a frog in boiling water, it will immediately jump out. But if you put the frog in cold water and slowly, slowly bring the water to a boil, it will simply sit there and boil alive.

Imagine you're the frog. You've been sitting there in the water, allowing yourself to become accustomed to very subtle rises in temperature. You're not consciously examining it. So you just accept the gradual boiling of life as if it's an intractable reality and the only place, or position, to be in. This is very much like looking at life through the lens of your limiting beliefs.

THE INNER GAME

Learning that you're experiencing your mood, not the world, is a fundamental shift in understanding. The most liberating aspect of this understanding is realising that when you're feeling low, you don't need to spend any time or energy trying to solve problems.

I came to realise that things which appeared to be problems in life, were often state-of-mind issues, rather than genuine problems. Once my state of mind rose to a higher level, either I knew what to do with the problem, or it no longer seemed like a problem.

This understanding also means that you don't need to work out why you are feeling the way you are. Your moods go up and down, and that's all you need to know.

I see it a bit like clouds in the sky. When you have perspective, you see the cloud. You see the white shapes in the blue sky, and you see the edges of the cloud. But when you're in an aeroplane and you fly through the cloud, you don't see the cloud because you're in it. All you see is white. Our thoughts are a lot like that. When you have perspective and a high level of awareness, you see the separateness between you and your thoughts. When you have a low level of awareness, you lose yourself in your thoughts.

You don't need to do anything with the clouds of thought; you just need to see that they are separate from you. We all have our own ways of dealing with unhelpful thoughts. I find it helpful to speak to a loved one when I'm feeling caught up in my head. I find that even the act of speaking my thoughts out loud to someone usually helps me to see through them. You might find it most helpful to go for a walk, take some exercise, or meditate. Anything that might help you not get so lost in your temporary low mood.

LEARNING WHEN NOT TO TAKE YOUR THINKING SERIOUSLY

It's not just the outside world that looks different depending on where we are on the ladder. The way that we experience ourselves changes, too.

When we're at the bottom of the ladder, things look very different to us. We have a phenomenon known as "autobiographical memory bias". This means that memories are filtered through our current internal state, which in turn means that happy memories, when viewed through the lens of a low mood, don't look quite as happy.

One of my clients was a junior doctor, and we had already had a few sessions together, so I was getting to know her

174

quite well. In a particular session, she came in feeling quite depressed. She told me that on reflection, she thought she had always been depressed. This surprised me, as in previous sessions, despite currently going through a tricky time, there was a general lightness about her, and she was usually very quick to smile. In short, I knew enough not to buy into her story about always being depressed.

I pointed this out to her, but she couldn't see past her current emotional state. Knowing how her current view was being filtered through the lens of her low mood, I invited her to bring up some pictures on her phone.

I asked her to look through them, and not just the ones that she thought would be good enough to post on social media, but all the photos she had taken of herself doing various things.

Within seconds, her shoulders dropped, she let out a breath, and the tension dropped from her face. She looked at me, smiled, and said, "Oh, yeah, I'm not normally depressed." Her entire experience changed in an instant.

She'd been having a low mood; she was down on one of the bottom rungs of the ladder, and had added to her internal experience the idea that "I'm always down here"/"I'm always depressed", therefore fixing her state as opposed to knowing there are other steps or rungs to climb, and different vantage points from which to view a situation.

Our present moment view of life is distorted by how we're feeling. It's like a trick of the mind, an illusion. Learning when not to trust your thinking is key to wellbeing and resilience.

If you know not to take your thinking so seriously when you're feeling low, anxious or stressed, then you won't get bogged down by life seeming more hard than usual and people seeming more threatening than they usually do. Low moods come and go but we can make them stick.

When you first wake up in the morning, you might feel lethargic for the first few minutes. Most of us find that this morning sleep inertia will pass quite quickly, so imagine looking at the day ahead through the lens of that temporary disorientation and tiredness. You picture all the things you have planned that day, like getting the kids ready for school, going for a run, work, and going out for dinner that evening. You likely won't feel like doing any of it in the moment because you're looking through the current feelings of grogginess.

Our moods can work the same way if we don't add too much to them with our thinking. I've heard people say that they know it will be a bad day the moment they wake up, based on their first feeling that morning. They make the mistake of "locking in" on their feelings as if they are a reliable indicator as to how they will feel later if they were only to be present and open to those feelings passing.

Imagine if you were just about to get on a ghost train. Whether you consciously know it or not, before the ride starts up, you're probably going to have already decided not to trust your perceptions for the duration of the ride. This is a helpful stance to take, as it means that when the skeletons fly over your carriage and actors dressed as zombies jump out yelling "boo", you won't take any of it too seriously.

I remember when I used to think it was just a fact that life was hard. Things were an almost constant struggle to me. I often felt exhausted from having to work hard to get through life, and it felt like I'd solve one problem, only to move straight onto the next. I was on the ghost train and I was convinced I saw… real ghosts.

What struck me the most was that every now and then, without circumstances seeming to change, I'd get a bit of a break from the struggle. It was like taking a holiday from what I assumed was just life, and I would step into a world that seemed more straightforward, and where I momentarily found peace. I'd experience what I thought was a high, a temporary relief from the truth of a hard life.

I also recall, however, occasionally sinking even lower at times, and finding life even more challenging. Little did I know this was simply the ladder of my moods.

There's a fundamental difference between thinking "I'm in a low mood **because** life is so hard", and "I'm in a bad mood, so life is **looking** hard to me in this moment."

The trick is never to believe anything you think when you're low.

It's just like if you've ever said something to someone when you're feeling hurt, you wouldn't mean it. Not believing what your thinking tells you when you're in a low mood, is key to allowing the mood to pass.

So, how do we get our low moods to pass quickly?

I'd like to explore the answer to this question by asking a different question: how would we keep ourselves in a low mood? Or perhaps, how would we make our mood even lower when already feeling low? Here are some possible ways:

- Wonder what's wrong with you
- Ruminate on why you're feeling the way you're feeling
- Worry that you'll always feel like this
- Dwell on other times you've felt like this
- Worry about how low you're going to get
- Analyse all the areas of your life looking for what's not going well

And these are just the things we do in our head! (Let alone how we sustain low moods with our actions and inactions).

All this thinking about a temporary low mood, which would pass on its own. But when we give it meaning, we add to it, and then suddenly, not only are we experiencing a low mood, but we're also experiencing the emotions that come with the negative story about the low mood. It feels depressing and burdensome to think that there's something wrong with you.

So now that we can answer the question of how to get our low mood to pass?

It's simple: don't do any of the above.

One of the most helpful questions that came to me once when I was struggling was this:

Who are you imagining you are right now?

Are you picturing yourself as someone who is confident, well-liked and funny? Or are you imagining yourself as someone to be not good enough, clumsy, inarticulate and just unlucky at life?

I would often find that when life seemed difficult or things weren't going the way I wanted, I was imagining something about myself that was both unhelpful and untrue. You might also find this question helpful when you're feeling stuck or unhappy.

INNATE WELLBEING

When I used to teach resilience building to my psychotherapy students, I would often draw a picture of a ladder on the board, and then a wavy line to represent our fluctuating moods. I would always draw a dotted line across the middle of the ladder to define the baseline of where our mood would naturally rest. How mistaken I was.

Due to my training, I'd always assumed that on this ladder, our baseline of mood would be somewhere in the middle. That we could go both up and down in mood, but that our resting state was halfway in between the top and bottom.

But what if our resting state was actually at the top of the ladder?

If we look at young children, we can see that as long as their needs are met, they generally maintain a high state of mood, accompanied by endless energy, creativity, natural intelligence, and enthusiasm for life. Our resting state isn't just a bit "meh", it's one of natural joy and pure peace.

Young children haven't taken a course on how to be happy or how to be present and enjoy their lives. This points to the truth of our wellbeing being our natural state. We just need to return to our natural way of being.

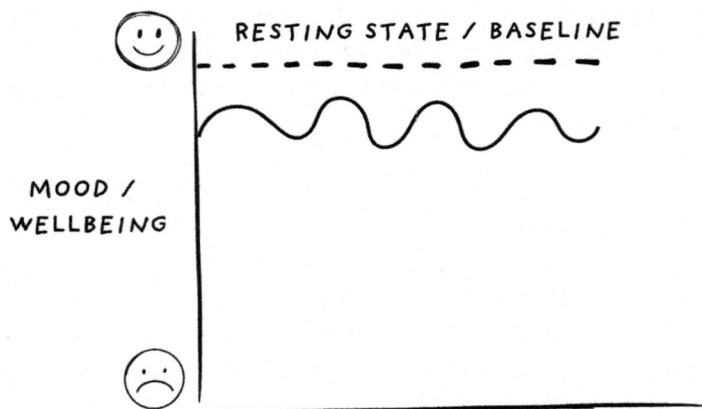

Innate and natural simply mean that we're not talking about a skill that needs to be learnt. Our wellbeing is already built in, as our default setting. It occurs to me that I've never had to teach my children to be present. They are born that way, and they haven't yet been conditioned out of it.

Children are naturally resilient, with confidence and a willingness to try anything. They are naturally engaged with whatever they are doing in the moment without too much thinking. Creativity, openness, compassion and curiosity are often present.

It's in our very nature to have good wellbeing. This means that wellbeing isn't something you need to learn; it's already there and remains constant. But we can think our way out of feeling it.

Until I realised the truth about our innate wellbeing, I had been teaching people that they needed to add things to their psychological toolkit in order to achieve a better state of mind and resilience. I would innocently but incorrectly teach them that they needed to think differently or behave differently in order to achieve their desired state.

But this doesn't make sense when you realise that resilience and wellbeing are built into us. They are there by default. We don't need to add anything.

I remember when I bought myself a guitar for the first time. The guy in the shop said that it was already tuned and that I didn't need to mess with it. However, I decided that I knew better, so when I got home, I played around with the strings, soon finding the guitar was way out of tune. I also found that the more I played with it, the worse it sounded.

I like to think that our wellbeing doesn't need any messing with. It's perfectly in tune as it is. High wellbeing is the standard setting. When we think too much about how we're feeling, or we make our low moods mean that there is something wrong with us, then we interfere with the natural correcting mechanism that lies within our wellbeing that we might call resilience – the ability to bounce back. Unlike the guitar however, we don't need to return to the shop to get it back to its default setting. We just need to leave it alone and it will reset itself.

I think that although stress, anxiety, and low mood states are natural, holding on to them is not. States of clarity, a light mood and the qualities that come with those states are our natural resting state.

This is why you can meet people in some dire circumstances, but who maintain a radiant sense of happiness and inner peace. Given that happiness, joy, peace, and wellbeing are our natural states, we don't need to look anywhere outside ourselves for them, we don't need to attain anything to get them, and we don't need to learn anything to be happy. We do, however, need to do a bit of unlearning!

Unlearning the idea that happiness is outside us. Unlearning what society tells us will make us happy. Unlearning that we should work hard and spend our money on things that will bring us some sense of meaning.

Rather than saying that you have to add anything to your life, or your thinking, I believe that it is more a case of subtraction. Subtracting the thinking you have that clouds over your wellbeing.

There's a brilliant video on YouTube called 'Happiness' by Steve Cutts; it's a fantastic little wake-up call that shows how we're so accustomed to seeking happiness outside ourselves that we forget to look in the one place it always is: inside. I encourage you to take a moment out of reading this and check out the video now.

There's something very comforting about knowing that peace is always there inside of you. Even if you can't feel it right now, it's there in your nature.

What I'm suggesting is that when you truly understand how our perception works, when you are away from your innate wellbeing, it will make sense for you not to take your thinking too seriously.

The more we do this, the quicker our wellbeing will rise, and we have clarity again. It's a self-correcting system, just like the way you don't need to help a beach ball float to the top of the water, our resilience works the same way as long as we don't interfere with it.

And just like you can hold a beach ball under the water, you can hold your wellbeing down with thought. Whenever you're thinking about something negative that seems more important to think about than to let go of, you're holding the beachball of your wellbeing underwater.

The next natural question might be, if it's true that our wellbeing and resilience are innate and natural, why aren't we in that state all the time? Especially when we can experience what seems like an ongoing low mood and anxiety?

The answer is that we unconsciously and innocently cover up our wellbeing through our thoughts. Because most of our thinking is outside of our awareness, we're likely thinking something that we don't even know we're thinking.

LETTING GO

Just as clouds obscure the sun, our wellbeing is often obscured by our thoughts. Instead of experiencing the warmth of our wellbeing, we usually feel thoughts like "I'm not good enough" or some other personal thinking that arises on top of our innate inner climate.

It might be a thought of "something's wrong", or "I can't be happy now, I'll be happy when... [fill in blank]".

'Most people treat the present moment as if it were an obstacle that they need to overcome. Since the present moment is life itself, it is an insane way to live.'
(Eckhart Tolle)

Thought is far more reaching than you realise. Seeing as our emotions stem from thought, thought is worth understanding enough to see through its illusory nature.

We don't feel circumstances or situations, we feel our thinking. Thought creates our experience, the content of our lives. We are only conscious of a tiny proportion of what we're thinking that creates our experience.

To know that we need to unlearn or decondition ourselves from the thinking we have that takes us out of our natural resting state is enough to spark your natural curiosity and intelligence, allowing you to let go of your thinking and rediscover your innate wellbeing.

'Nature needs no help, just no interference.'
(B. J. Palmer, Chiropractor)

As I've spoken about earlier, in the context of my own children, whilst toddlers can exhibit what might appear to be extreme moods, they tend to pass quickly. They can go from happy to sad, back to happy, to angry in a matter of moments, but they don't get stuck in any one place.

Have you ever had an experience where you and your partner are upset with each other and you're both sharing your frustrated thoughts, only for one of you to accidentally break the low mood and smile? You then might feel compelled to stay in a bad mood, or you might let it go. Sometimes we hold onto our low mood or frustration on purpose.

This is about choosing. The higher our level of awareness, the more choice we have.

The more we learn to let go of thoughts as a choice, the quicker low moods will pass without much drama, as we're not perpetuating the mood with actions or more negative thinking. Instead of creating a vicious cycle, we cut off the negativity at its source.

I've learned from my own experience that the worst thing I can do when I'm in a low mood is to start analysing my circumstances as to the cause of my low mood. The problem with doing that is that we will view the story of our circumstances (and our future) through the lens of the low mood that we are currently in.

It would be like you're getting a depressed commentator giving you a rundown on how things are going.

If you look at the work of Dr Jill Bolte Taylor, she has shown that emotions typically subside within 90 seconds when left unattended. If the emotion lasts longer, it is being perpetuated by thought.

'After 90 seconds, the initial chemical reaction is over. If you still feel fear, anger, anxiety, or any other emotion,

it's not your physiology that's fuelling it – it's your own thoughts re-stimulating the chemical changes. These thoughts construct a feedback loop which re-activate the chemical response and embed the emotion deeper. So you could say that our uniquely human ability to think makes it possible for us to get stuck in the emotional loop.'
(Dr Jill Bolte Taylor)

When we are further down the ladder of moods than we'd like to be, the best way to exacerbate it is to add to it with criticism, judgment, or any actions that feed that emotional state.

Most of us assume that if we're feeling low, then we're doing something wrong. We start to either look outside ourselves, and analyse our various circumstances for the source of our unfulfillment. Or we blame ourselves for feeling down and think that something in our psychology must be flawed.

I know this first-hand. After studying psychology for ten years and being called an "expert in CBT", I thought I knew enough never to feel anxious or low again. So, when I inevitably experienced a low mood, I would exacerbate it by thinking, "What am I doing wrong? I really must be broken."

It was like hitting myself while I was already down with a self-development stick that said, "I should know better". What I came to realise was that if I wanted to keep my mood low, this was effective. However, these judgments were also the only thing that kept my mood low. When I learned just to let go of my thoughts, my low mood would pass very quickly.

MOODS AND ACTION

Your behaviours and activities reflect how you feel on the inside.

Because of the way our personal reality works, we see, think, listen, and act from our inner state.

What we do when we're in a high mood tends to reinforce our state of being. When we're feeling good, we tend to want to eat well, be kind to others, and generally nurture our high level of wellbeing with actions that complement us.

When we're feeling low, we're at risk of reinforcing our low mood state. I know when I'm feeling a bit low, I want to reach for some comfort food, put off my work, skip the gym, and withdraw from people. You, too, might find that when you're not feeling how you want to feel, you neglect the things that usually seem pretty crucial to you. Perhaps you shut yourself off, neglect talking to your family or friends, stop doing your morning yoga, stop reading, journaling, or buying the best food produce you'd normally buy; perhaps you wallow in front of the TV or Netflix, or comfort yourself by going shopping for things you really don't need.

But we don't have to act how we think or feel. Imagine if we just acted according to our feelings. Just because we feel like snapping at someone doesn't mean we have to.

One of my clients was an athlete who would get up at 5 a.m. to train. When I asked her how she was able to do that consistently, she replied simply, "I just don't pay any attention to how I'm feeling when I first wake up."

When we have a vision or a commitment, how we feel moment to moment becomes less important than that which we're aiming for.

REFLECTION

Take a moment to reflect on what you make it mean when you're in a low mood. (About yourself, others, and life?)

What about when you are high in mood? How do other people seem then? What does life look like to you? How do you imagine others see you?

KEY INSIGHTS:

◆ Don't believe what you think when you're in a low mood.

◆ Don't make big decisions when you're low.

◆ Life looks very different depending on your current mood state.

◆ Our default state is one of wellbeing. We don't need to do anything to have wellbeing, other than to let go of any unhelpful thoughts.

◆ Thinking is the only thing that gets in the way of our innate wellbeing.

FROM INSIGHT TO ACTION

What actions or habits would you stop doing when you feel low, anxious or stressed? And how might these reducing these behaviours help your mood pass quicker?

CHAPTER 9

THE LADDER OF CONSCIOUSNESS

'No problem can be solved from the same level of
consciousness that created it.'
Albert Einstein

In 2016 I had an enlightenment experience. Through a deep and profound insight into understanding my own true nature and the nature of all human beings, I sank into a deep well of joy and connection. Everything changed for me, and for a period of around two to three months, I walked around in a near-constant state of deep peace, accompanied by a felt sense of connection with everyone and everything. I was in a consistent state of flow, and it seemed as though I knew the answers to all of life's problems.

I found that when others came to me with their struggles, I could see the root cause of all their suffering. It seemed that all they needed to do to be free of their problems was to separate themselves from their own struggle. To disidentify from being the one who is clouded by negative thought, to the one who sits behind, in the background, and simply observes the struggle. This would often be articulated by me saying to clients: "Just watch it".

Whilst there was no doubt in my mind that this was the obvious solution, the extent to which others saw this depended on their own level of consciousness.

THOUGHT AND CONSCIOUSNESS

When we have a high level of awareness and we're high up on the ladder of consciousness, we see through the illusion of thought to a deeper understanding of how our mind works. When we have a low level of consciousness, on a lower rung of the ladder, thought doesn't appear to be thought; instead, it looks like real life.

It looks a bit like this to me…

Imagine you'd just arrived home, and you see your partner watching television in the lounge. You're about to say hi when you notice what's on the screen, and instead, you gasp.

You see the city of London in a cloud of fire, dust, and rubble, in absolute chaos at what appears to be a large explosion in the middle of the city. What surprises you almost as much as what you see on TV is how calm your partner looks as they observe what's on the screen.

"How are you so calm!?" You exclaim.

"What?" They say with what seems like genuine curiosity.

"The news!" You reply in earnest.

"The news?" They say, looking confused at your level of emotion.

It's then that you realise that they are, in fact, just watching a disaster movie.

It's the thoughts that don't appear to be thoughts that create the problems.

The higher your level of consciousness, the more you see through the illusory nature of the imagined catastrophe. The great thing about this is that it doesn't take any tools or techniques to see the truth of this. It doesn't even take any time. What it takes is seeing things from a higher level of consciousness, which can happen in a moment.

When I had my enlightenment experience, I felt myself jump to a higher level of consciousness. When I would tell people to "just watch it," what I meant was that they needed to raise their level of consciousness above the problem, and then, from there, the problem and struggle would dissipate.

For example, from time to time, my client Emily would become upset when she thought a group of friends was excluding her from conversations. She would often feel as if she were consigned to the sidelines, not included in conversations. She wanted to be more involved and not feel so left out.

When Emily saw more about the nature of thought and consciousness and how this worked for her, she realised that feeling ignored was a familiar pattern for her, and that it had started in childhood. Emily often felt left out as a child, and so it was somewhat usual for her to feel like she didn't quite fit in.

When Emily saw the pattern for what it was, her level of consciousness rose above it. She saw at a deep level that it was in her **thinking** that she was being left out. It was then that she saw for herself the difference between a real-life problem and a problem that only existed in thought.

The problem then looked less real to her, and she realised that her friends were not intentionally excluding her from specific conversations, and that it didn't need addressing. With this insight, Emily naturally felt more herself and was able to engage with her friends with ease, deepening the connection between them.

If Emily hadn't seen through the illusion of her thinking, she would have been trying to solve the problem from the level of actually being left out, and the problem would have been unsolvable from that level.

Consciousness is like a blank screen. A screen on which we see our thinking. And the more conscious we are, the more aware we become that our thinking is our own, manufactured, and not an objective reality. The less conscious we are, the more lost in thought we become, because our thinking appears less distinct and more like the way things are.

Low levels of consciousness are not a problem, but life can become tricky to navigate when you expend your energy and efforts trying to solve problems of thought that aren't actually problems at all.

Another way to see this understanding is that thought and consciousness work like a seesaw. When your level of consciousness comes up, thought comes down. It looks like this to me:

THOUGHTS DON'T APPEAR
SO FIXED AND CONCRETE

AWARENESS

THOUGHT

Conscious awareness is always present, and when you are higher in consciousness than the personal thinking you're having, thought never looks like a problem, because you can see it for what it is – made up, and transient.

In contrast, when your level of presence is low, thought doesn't look like thought, and we can get stuck. If you weren't particularly conscious, you could potentially go your whole life assuming that you were seeing things just the way they are. But how you see things is not fixed, because you're seeing it with the malleability of thought, and so it is always changeable.

The more conscious you are, the more you see what's thought and what's not. In other words, the more present you become, the clearer your mind, and the less you identify with your habitual, manufactured thinking, and the more you identify with the awareness of that which is before thought.

THOUGHT DOESN'T LOOK LIKE THOUGHT - IT LOOKS LIKE LIFE

If I were to tell you that you're going to win the lottery tonight, you probably wouldn't get that excited because you wouldn't **believe** that was true. It's easy to see that the thought about winning the lottery is just a thought. Thoughts can't make you feel anything if you know that they're just thoughts and not reality.

But what about thoughts that don't look like thoughts?

Many of us are living in our heads, believing things that aren't true. If you've ever tried telling someone to walk under a ladder if they fully believe it's bad luck, you soon see this. We also, at times, get lost in thoughts that something bad is going to happen, as we feel the associated emotion to the extent that we believe that thought.

THE POWER OF THOUGHT

Just for a moment, try to forget everything you think you

know about thought. Thought is much bigger than simply the content of your thinking.

The reason you are able to think is due to the creative power of thought, as Sydney Banks called Universal Thought.

Thinking is just what happens to go through your mind in terms of words and images. Universal Thought is the energy from which we create our very own unique experience of life. Thought and consciousness are what we use to make our reality.

Thought is powerful stuff. The placebo effect demonstrates just how powerful thought can be when our brain can tell our body what we believe, and our body can bring about the actual physical changes because of the power of our belief.

In one study, for example, a group of depressed people were given a pill with nothing in it other than sugar, but were told it was an antidepressant. Another group were given an antidepressant. Both groups showed very similar recovery rates, the conclusion being that the belief in the pill working, actually brought about mood changes.

Another study found that if we think a sugar pill contains a pain-alleviating chemical, our pain subsides to a similar degree as if we were taking the actual drug.

Other studies have shown similar powerful effects, all of which are attributable to the power of thought, triggering changes in physiology.

I remember being in my early twenties and out drinking with some friends. I had the idea of buying one of our group alcohol-free beers for the evening without them knowing, in order to test out the placebo effect! By the end of the evening, we'd all had several drinks, apart from this one person, who actually only had one alcoholic lager. Amazingly, he was as drunk as the rest of us! Even when we eventually (in hysterics) told him that he'd been alcohol free all night. He still to this day doesn't believe us when we tell him he'd only had one beer!

Your beliefs create your reality more than you likely realise.

Everything we see, hear, taste, touch and smell is experienced by us via the mental activity that we might call thought.

We can create any experience that occurs to us via the power of thought. Whenever you use your thinking to scare yourself, that's how you're using thought in that moment. Whenever you're looking at your children and feeling love, that's how you're using thought in that moment.

When you think of the past, you're not merely remembering it; you're creating it in your awareness right now - that's thought. When you imagine the future, you're simply creating an image, and (most likely accompanied by feelings), using the power of thought.

There is no experience outside of thought because it takes the energy of thought to be aware of something. In other words, you can't observe something independent of thought. We experience not the outside world, but instead, our own thought-created representation of the world. The way you see yourself and the world is via the power of thought.

We refer to rose-tinted glasses or dark-tinted spectacles. We say, "You know such and such, they're walking around in their own little bubble". Well, your own thought works like this, too, like a pair of old-fashioned 3D glasses, tinted red and green; they colour everything you see.

For another metaphor, thought is like soft clay, and it's the type of clay that's always soft, it's always malleable. We might incorrectly assume that once we've formed a sculpture out of this clay, it sets and is no longer pliable. But this 'thought-clay' is a special clay, re-moldable, re-purposeable, capable of forming new exciting shapes.

We fix a thought in our consciousness when we stop seeing the inherent softness and malleability. When we deeply understand thought, we see this pliability present in every moment.

THE POWERLESSNESS OF THOUGHT

As powerful as thought is, it's only powerful when we don't see it for what it is.

Thought creates our reality, but only when we don't see it's thought. When we see thought for what it is, (energy, malleable, creative in nature), we don't get lost in it.

Consider that you have thinking all the time that you don't act on, that you don't take seriously.

When you have a thought that you don't see is a thought, you might call that a belief. We live inside our beliefs and look out through the lens of that belief. Just like when you have a superstition and you don't see it's just thought, you refuse to walk under a ladder, for fear of something bad happening, not realising that the world doesn't work like that.

The result of seeing how thought works, is that if we know that we're looking through a lens, then we're less attached to what we're seeing. There's then less need to try and fix things on the outside, and less worry and concern with our current perspective.

For me, I've come to see that my world is a projection of my thoughts. I know that how I'm perceiving things isn't an objective measure of life or circumstances because I'm perceiving life through my thoughts. Whatever the circumstances I happen to be in right now, I will have a subjective experience about it. My story of life, is **a** story, not **the** story.

When we see through and beyond thought, we usually touch the space before thought. You know that space. We all do. We might call it the space of meditation. When you're in this space you feel peaceful, content, creative, free, and although anything is possible.

CONSCIOUSNESS AND MOOD

Just like we all go up and down in mood, we all go up and down in levels of consciousness all the time.

We all have times where we are low in consciousness and we're on autopilot, driving past our turn, or finishing off a packet of crisps without really being aware.

We also have times when we're at a high level of consciousness, where we are aware, and we know that we are aware. At times like these, you also see through any thoughts that might bother you when you're at a lower level of consciousness. Going up and down is as natural as the sun rising and setting.

Another helpful thing to remember is that our mood is distinct from our level of consciousness, which means that we can experience a low mood with either a low or high level of consciousness. You can also be in a high mood with high consciousness, and a high mood with low consciousness. It looks a bit like this:

HIGH AWARENESS   HIGH MOOD

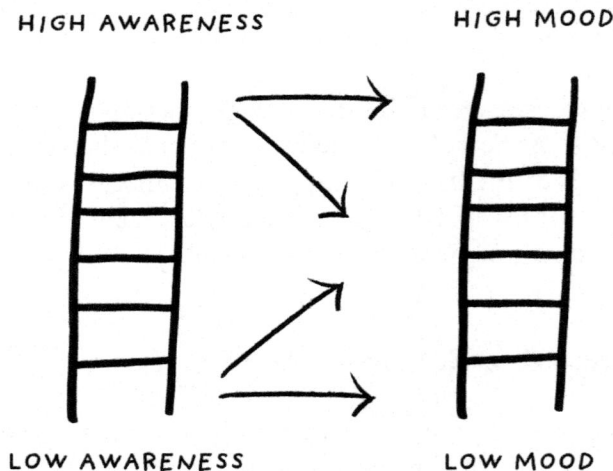

LOW AWARENESS   LOW MOOD

What this might look like is being low down on the ladder of moods and being acutely aware that you are in that low mood state. This is in contrast to you being in a low mood and not being fully aware of how low you are and how it might be impacting you and your perception.

Picture a postman on his postal round-the sky looks grey, the houses, streets and people all look grey, too; he can barely bring himself to finish his round as it all seems so depressing, so it takes him twice as long. Whereas another postman on his round also sees the same greyness and feels glum, but - knowing that it's merely his state of mind at the moment and part of his thinking - ploughs on through the round, knowing it will pass, and makes it back home in the same amount of time he normally would.

When we're low in mood, but in a high state of consciousness, we're less reactive because we're fully aware that we're just experiencing our thoughts in the moment, and life isn't as bad as it might appear at the time. When you know this, you're also less likely to take too much notice of your urges, thoughts and feelings in lower states because you know they will pass. The postman with a low mood but a high level of consciousness will wait for his mood to pass, whereas the postman with a low mood and a low level of consciousness may ignore anyone he comes into contact with, fantasise about quitting his job, or even quit his job.

Knowing about temporary mood states and how they shape how we see life is actually one of the most freeing things I have learnt over my two decades of studying human potential and development. I used to think it was my job to feel good all the time. It was exhausting! In other words, I thought the game of life was about being happy and that if I wasn't happy, I was doing something wrong.

*'Everyone is doing the best they can, given the thinking
they have that looks real to them.'*
(Sydney Banks)

This sort of pressure I used to put on myself reminds me of when a client of mine had a heart attack. Following his operation, the doctor advised him to avoid stress at all costs. When my client called to tell me the news, he then followed by saying that the most stressful thing of all is now thinking that he needs to avoid all stress! He wasn't joking, and became hypersensitive to any signs of stress. The problem with trying to remove stress with stress, is that it works about as well as trying to remove superglue with superglue. That is to say... it doesn't.

What I've come to see for myself is that it's not my job to be happy all the time. And when I let go of the goal of trying to be high up on either my mood or my level of consciousness, something remarkable happens. Both raise all by themselves and I spend more time being happy.

Why is this?

Because this is how we're made. To have high levels of both wellbeing and awareness. When we don't let our thinking get in the way, both come back to their resting state.

We can make passing moments of stress, anxiety, low mood or unhappiness mean something. We can hold onto them in the hope of fixing them. But the more we hold onto them, the more they linger. If we instead let go of our thinking, we return to our innate wellbeing.

Here's something that you probably already know:

You can't control your thoughts.

I bet you've tried.

But we *can* control how seriously we take our thoughts.

Something I've learned that truly helps me is the following:

Knowing how something works doesn't mean that it doesn't work on you.

Just because I know ice is slippery, doesn't mean that when I walk on it, I won't slip. I used to make the mistake of assuming incorrectly that because I understood my psychology, I would never feel down, stressed, or anxious again.

However, we are human beings, and we feel our thinking. Seeing as we can't control our thinking, we can't control how we feel. But we don't have to add to the feeling by making it mean that there's something wrong with us, like I used to.

REFLECTION

What do you spend most of your time being aware of? In other words, what are the things that take up the most space in your consciousness?

When has something looked like a real-life problem to you one moment, and then your consciousness has risen, and you've seen it in a completely different way?

How can you personally tell when your level of consciousness is high?

What tells you when it's low?

If consciousness is a blank screen, we paint consciousness with thought in each moment, and we see that thought reflected back to us.

We have the potential and the ability to paint any thought onto this empty screen and to let it go, or to keep it there in our awareness. The more meaning we add to a thought, the more likely we are to keep it alive in our consciousness. If we don't think something is important, we tend to stop thinking about it and let it go.

Some of the things we learned to think are helpful to keep thinking, such as our name and where we live. However, some things aren't that helpful, and yet, on some level, we must think they are important because we keep thinking about them.

A client of mine, Mike, came to me because he was struggling to maintain relationships. He was stuck in the past with too much thinking that was getting in the way of maintaining intimacy. In this conversation, Mike saw through what he thought was a valid reason to keep himself safe.

Mike: I just can't seem to commit to anyone. I'm okay with getting close initially, but then I just find it too much, so I leave. I can feel it happening again now with my current girlfriend.

Chris: Does this happen in every relationship?

Mike: Yes, and I always seem to get scared after about five months in.

Chris: What do you think is the thing that changes over time for your feelings to change like that?

Mike: I don't know, I know it's me, I just don't know what it is in me.

Chris: Well, the only thing I know it can be is your thinking. That's where our feelings come from. So, what must be going through your mind that scares you?

Mike: It's when I'm starting to fall for someone. I just feel like when someone really gets to know me, the real me, they couldn't possibly love me. I remember something my Mum said to me once, and it comes up in my mind when I'm feeling the intimacy building in a relationship.

Chris: It sounds like whatever your Mum said was hurtful.

Mike: Yes, and I've spoken about it in counselling. Do we need to talk through it again?

Chris: No, we don't need to bring that back up for you. This type of conversation is very different. I'd actually suggest that you don't need to keep thinking about what your Mum said.

Mike: That's a relief, but how do I not think about it?

Chris: Well, can I ask you a different question?

Mike: Sure.

Chris: If I could help you never think about it again, would you really want me to help you?

Mike: Of course.

Chris: Ok, great, so you're pleased to let that thought go? You fully believe that the thought doesn't serve you?

Mike: Oh, well, I guess it protects me.

Chris: Does it? Or does it hurt you?

Mike: Yes, it does hurt me. But I'm scared to let it go.

Chris: That's because you're believing that no one can love you. If you were really in a world where no one could love you, then it would make perfect sense to keep people away. But you're not in that world. In my opinion, you possess complete peace and love within you. All you need to do is get out of its way.

Mike: And I'm getting in the way with my thinking?

Chris: Yes. Your thinking is the only thing that can keep down your peace and innate wellbeing.

Mike: But what my Mum said hurt so much. I don't know if I can stop thinking about it.

Chris: I know. But what's more hurtful right now? Something that your Mum said thirty or forty years ago, or that you keep thinking it?

Mike: Oh my God. It's me. I'm the one hurting myself. [Sighs relief].

Chris: Yes, and you were innocently doing it, but you don't need to keep thinking it now that you know it's not important. We can keep the past alive in our consciousness through thought, but we can let it go anytime it no longer serves us.

Mike: Oh. Wow.

Chris: What is it?

Mike: I know this sounds weird and sudden, but... as soon as you said that, I actually just felt something shift, like... I actually just had a rush of love for my girlfriend.

We constantly have a blank screen available to us in each moment. There is pure potential in consciousness. Sometimes we fill our consciousness with love and possibilities. Sometimes we fill it with fear and worry. The more you paint it with hurt and anxiety, the more you feel hurt and anxious. The more you paint it with love, the more you feel love.

HOW DO WE RAISE OUR LEVEL OF CONSCIOUSNESS?

I've found that trying to raise my level of consciousness doesn't work very well. It's very easy to slip into a way of thinking that you need to do something, or **add** something to your life, in order for you to be happy. However, I'm suggesting a different, more subtractive approach, unlike almost any other.

Given that having a high level of awareness is our natural resting state, the more helpful question is usually, what am I doing to lower my level of consciousness?

Consciousness, by its nature, goes up and down, and if we let it, it will return to where it naturally rests. One thing I found to be particularly helpful is to let the various levels come and go without resistance. If there's no resistance to the lower levels, we don't get stuck.

When I'm low in consciousness, I have the choice to either struggle and resist it or to let go. When I struggle, it tends to keep it low. If I try to fix it myself, this acts as a form of resistance and can lower my consciousness even further. When I see the truth, that nothing is wrong, and I simply let go and allow things to be as they are, my level tends to rise as quickly as I leave it alone.

It's easy to let go of thoughts.

We do it all the time.

It's just that usually there's resistance to letting go of specific thoughts. It's much easier to let go of thoughts when you stop giving yourself reasons not to hold onto them. When you do drop them, you find yourself here, now, in the present moment, along with a feeling of deep peace and aliveness.

What I'd say is that if any thoughts are getting in the way of your happiness and freedom, do your best to let go of your thinking. This raises your level of consciousness above any negative thinking you may have. This is all you ever need to do.

To sum it up;

Don't be the thought, be the one observing the thought. Don't be the habit or behaviour, be the one observing it.

KEY INSIGHTS:

- ◆ We have varying levels of consciousness that fluctuate, independent of our mood.
- ◆ The higher our level of consciousness, the more aware we are that our thoughts are not reality, and that 'thought problems' don't need to be solved.
- ◆ The more present we are, the more we tap into our natural inner wisdom, and the more we see through our thought-created reality.
- ◆ Being in a high state of awareness means we are less reactive when in a low mood. We see that the low mood is just due to our experience of our thoughts, and is temporary.
- ◆ We can't control our thoughts, but we can control how seriously we take those thoughts.

◆ To raise our level of consciousness, simply allow
things to be as they are and don't resist the low
levels.

FROM INSIGHT TO ACTION

*Think of a behaviour that you'd like to change.
Instead of trying to change it, see if you can
bring a sense of freedom to it. In other words,
play with the idea of doing the same thing, but
coming from a place of pure freedom. Then see
how that changes your experience.*

CHAPTER 10

WHAT DO YOU WANT?

'A ship is safe in harbour – but that's not what ships are for.'
John A. Shedd

I was 26 years old when I fully woke to what I wanted in life. I was a leader in a successful corporate job, managing a large team. It was good money, I was well-liked and respected. All of it looked good on paper. But I was burnt out and deeply unfulfilled.

I was then lucky enough to find a mentor who asked me what I actually wanted to do in my life.

The thing about this question was that it wasn't just one made in passing. My mentor looked at me with a serious expression on his face and asked me: "What do you really want?" I heard him, and I answered, "Well... I'm fascinated about how to get the best out of people."

"Tell me more." He said.

"I love getting the most out of my team, but sometimes they get stuck, and I'd love to learn more about what makes people tick."

"That's the study of psychology. Why don't you go and study that?"

"I'd love to! I have a friend who is doing a degree in psychology, and I'm always asking them about what they're learning. It's fascinating."

"So?"

"I can't do that. I'm too old!"

"You're 26, not 96."

"Well, yes, but I also can't afford to pay for university, and I'm not intelligent enough."

This mentor changed the trajectory of my life by helping me see past my fears and doubts and allowing me to get in touch with my real wants. At the end of the conversation, it felt like a calling I just couldn't ignore. It turned out that my wanting was so strong that within a couple of weeks of speaking with him, I had my manager agree to let me go part-time whilst I studied a full-time degree in psychology.

My desire was also strong enough that when the university rejected my application, I called them up and told them that I had never been more sure of anything in my life and would graduate top of the class. I spoke from the heart, and I couldn't believe the words that were coming out of my mouth. I had never been so bold in any of my communication. I was as surprised as they were about my level of certainty, and even more so when the course director said, "ok, you're in!"

When I think of it now, I loved every minute of my studies in psychology, and all it took was for someone to ask me, sincerely, what I wanted.

WHAT DO YOU WANT?

The time we live in is not the Industrial Revolution, where we're obliged to work jobs just to pay the bills. As such, I believe we are all entitled to follow our own unique passions and gifts and live a life of inspiration and authenticity.

I've met swimming teachers who love what they do and swimming teachers who can't stand the very same job. I've worked with doctors who never wanted to be doctors and who dream of quitting, but can't because it would be seen as failing. I've met joyful checkout staff who bring a smile to each and every customer's face. I've met builders who love building houses and builders who would rather be pursuing their dreams of opening their own restaurant.

I fully believe that if everyone followed their hearts, with the passion and inspiration that is natural to them, things would work out harmoniously in the end. We'd still have people to build our houses and serve us drinks if we wanted to go to a restaurant for dinner. There would still be therapists who loved doing therapy (albeit we'd need fewer of them!). We'd still have people who would enjoy landscaping our gardens, lawyers who were passionate about societal rules, and even politicians who'd strive to bring world peace and end world hunger.

Consider the following story:

One day, a fisherman was lying on a beautiful beach, with his fishing pole propped up in the sand and his solitary line cast out into the sparkling blue surf. He was enjoying the warmth of the afternoon sun and the prospect of catching a fish.

About that time, a businessman came walking down the beach, trying to relieve some of the stress of his workday. He noticed the fisherman sitting on the beach and decided to find out why this fisherman was fishing instead of working harder to make a living for himself and his family.

"You aren't going to catch many fish that way," said the businessman to the fisherman. "You should be working rather than lying on the beach!"

The fisherman looked up at the businessman, smiled and replied, "And what will my reward be?"

"Well, you can get bigger nets and catch more fish!" was the businessman's answer. "And then what will my reward be?" asked the fisherman, still smiling. The businessman replied, "You will make money and you'll be able to buy a boat, which will then result in larger catches of fish!"

"And then what will my reward be?" asked the fisherman again.

The businessman was beginning to get a little irritated with the fisherman's questions. "You can buy a bigger boat, and hire some people to work for you!" he said.

215

"And then what will my reward be?" repeated the *fisherman.*

The businessman was getting angry. "Don't you understand? You can build up a fleet of fishing boats, sail all over the world, and let all your employees catch fish for you!"

Once again, the fisherman asked, "And then what will my reward be?"

The businessman was red with rage and shouted at the fisherman, "Don't you understand that you can become so rich that you will never have to work for your living again! You can spend all the rest of your days sitting on this beach, looking at the sunset. You won't have a care in the world!"

The fisherman, still smiling, looked up and said, "And what do you think I'm doing right now?"

(Adapted from a story by Heinrich Böll)

We can all be that fisherman (and if we enjoy growing businesses, we can do that too!)

The question is, why aren't we already simply following our dreams? What if it was natural to just follow our hearts desires?

YOUR INNER COMPASS

A lot of people find that because they've been living in a mind-made prison, they haven't looked to see what they want, or if what they want is possible.

216

One of my clients, Dave, wanted to start his own business, but he was working in a company he had no interest in. Dave described his work as soul-destroying, but it paid well, so he couldn't leave. Dave dreamed of starting a business built around his passion, but to him, it was a dream and not a possibility.

When I asked Dave why it wasn't possible, he shrugged his shoulders as if it was already obvious. He'd never actually looked to see if his ideas could realistically transform into a viable business. He was living in a world of limitation, a world where he couldn't possibly earn enough money by following his heart and passion.

Dave came to see me because he wanted me to help him find fulfilment with work. I asked him where in his life he did feel fulfilled.

Dave: I have a lovely home, wife and kids.

Chris: And how did you create that?

Dave: What do you mean?

Chris: Well, before you met your now wife, did you make a mental list of what type of woman would be possible for you to marry?

Dave: Oh, well, I didn't really think about it. I guess I just did what made me happy.

Chris: So you feel happy in that area of your life, because you followed your happiness?

Dave: Yes. But how could that work with my career?

Chris: Why wouldn't it work? As far as I can tell, that's exactly the way it works. How else could you find fulfilment other than by following what makes you feel happy and fulfilled?

Dave: But what about earning enough money?

Chris: What about these inspiring people you follow? Don't they earn enough from doing what they love?

Dave: Well, yes, but…

Dave had seen enough and knew enough by then not to bother finishing the sentence. Anything that came out of his mouth next would have been a thought tinged by self-doubt or anxiety. He was now in touch with possibility.

FUTURE
HAPPINESS

PRESENT MOMENT
HAPPINESS

If you want to create happiness, you must follow your present-moment happiness. If you want inspiration for your future, you have to follow the inspiration you have now. It's like a compass, you can't necessarily see the end goal, but you can head in the direction it's pointing you. In this case, the needle points you towards what you currently want in the form of desire, excitement, and inspiration.

A WAKE-UP CALL

I heard a story once from Michaell Neill and I'll recount it here as best as I can remember it:

Imagine you've died and you're on your way up to heaven. You meet a couple of angels at the gates of heaven, and they say, "Before we let you in, would you like to have a tour of the life you lived?"

"Why not?" You say.

The angels take you along a corridor of doors, and each door they open contains an immersive replay of parts of your life. You see yourself as a baby, you watch your first day of school, your graduation, your first kiss, and all the other big events.

You notice that you've looked in every door but one. You ask the angels what's behind that door, and the angels quickly glance at each other and look almost worried or sad. One replies, "There's nothing in there you'd want to see".

Your curiosity gets the better of you, and you ask again what's in there. The angels assure you that you're best off not looking, but you open the door anyway.

You can't believe your eyes. You see yourself having the most wonderful life, full of joy, love, and connection. You have everything you could possibly imagine, and your days are filled with laughter and bliss.

You come away, closing the door with tears in your eyes, and ask, "What was that? Heaven?"

The angels look at you sadly, and one replies, "That's the life you could have had if you followed your dreams".

When I tell that story to my clients, some cry, some shift in their seats, and some say something like "right, let's go, let's make this happen!"

OBSTACLES TO WANTING

Sometimes, as soon as you get in touch with your desires, your doubts and fears flood in so quickly that you almost lose your awareness of what you want. When this happens, it's not the wanting or desire that feels bad; it's the idea that you can't have your desire that feels bad.

In the group workshops I run, I sometimes have the participants do an exercise where they draw a picture of and write down on a poster what they want their life to look like and to be about. Interestingly, at this point, some people begin to look excited, and some look sad. Since the exercise is about daydreaming about what you'd love, I ask them why they look miserable. The answer is always some variation of not deserving it or not being able to have it.

Then I have the participants write down on a piece of clear, transparent paper why they believe they haven't already created their dream life, or can't do so. This is where they become aware of their limiting beliefs and habitual thinking that gets in the way of them following their passions.

I have them hold their tracing paper over the poster they've drawn of their dream life. This is when they see that they are looking at what's possible for themselves, but through a lens of limitation. They then realise that they are feeling the feelings of fear and doubt, instead of potential or possibility.

When we remove the tracing paper, they feel the feelings of wanting what they want. It's a powerful exercise, and people start to see that they can either choose to follow their fears or follow their dreams.

When I ask people what they want, they don't usually answer. They usually tell me what they don't want. They say, "I don't want stress and anxiety," or "I don't want to be burnt out." Some might say, "I don't want to be single anymore", or "I don't want to be married". But none of that speaks to what you do want; that's what you *don't* want.

Sometimes when I ask what they want, clients tell me what they think they should want. They might say, "Well, I guess I want my health", or "I suppose I should go for a promotion at work", or "I want to be successful", without even looking at what success means to them. "But that's not what you want, is it?" I say, "That's what you think you *should* want".

Occasionally, when I ask someone what they want, they tell me what they think is possible for themselves. "Well, I think I could probably grow my business to this level", or "I guess I could cope with the situation better". But that's not what you want; that's what you think is *possible*.

What you want is just what you want.

REFLECTION

If you put aside what you don't want, or what you think you should want, or what you think is possible, what do you simply want?

What would you love your life to be like?

What would be nice to do right now?

What would you just really like for yourself?

What does your heart long for?

The reason I've included this chapter here about getting in touch with what you want, and not earlier in the book, is that I often don't ask my clients what they want straight away. They usually either don't know what they want or are so caught up in survival mode that they think it's irrelevant.

Hopefully, by now, you'll be more in touch with what's possible, who you are, and where your experience is coming from. And given this, you're now in a better place to consider what you want and to pursue your desires.

FEAR AND DOUBT

Whenever you pursue your dreams, the bad news is that anxiety and self-doubt will come along with you. The good news is that so will your wanting. Wanting is powerful. People climb mountains, swim oceans, or give away kidneys to save someone they love, all because of desire.

Wanting is a feeling, and it's a strong feeling when you're in touch with it. It acts as a force on your heart and soul and will pull you through any challenge that gets in the way.

It's much easier to deal with anxiety and doubt when you see that they are just thoughts. It's easy to dismiss these thoughts when your vision of what's possible is strong enough to pull you through the scary thinking that often accompanies you.

One of the things I find that gets people stuck the most, is assessing the risk of what they will do *if* they fail. I remember once having to do a risk assessment for work, and it scared the hell out of me until I realised what was happening. I was picturing all the worst things that could possibly happen, and I was feeling the feelings from those imagined disasters.

I realised that this risk assessing was what some people habitually do for everything in their lives, and we call that worry. Worry doesn't feel good and can be paralysing.

While risk assessing is sometimes necessary from a practical standpoint (from an insurance perspective, for example), it's worth remembering that practically planning for something going wrong is very different from passively worrying about what might go wrong.

One of the things that happens with worry is that we tend to imagine the worst possible outcome, and then don't go any further in our imagining. It's as if life just stops there at the moment of catastrophe. But that's only how it works in our imagination. What typically happens is we imagine ourselves speaking in public, voice trembling, palms sweaty, vision blurred, people laughing at us, and people thinking less of us. And then the image stops there, as if it's the end. But it isn't the end. It's just the limits of what our anxious thinking has to say. Because when it comes down to it...

You can either follow your heart or you can follow your fears.

I caught myself when writing this book saying to Emma, "What if it only sells twenty copies?" It was obvious that it was my self-doubt speaking. And what am I going to follow, a thought of anxiety... or my passion? If you're reading this, you know the answer!

Why wouldn't you follow your heart, too?

CHOICE POINTS

It's never too late to follow the things you desire or want. You can change course at any time and feel the instant gratification of living into your happiness and desires right now. The only thing that would ever stop you from doing that is… a negative thought.

SELF-DOUBT
ANXIETY

INSPIRATION
EXCITMENT

CHOICE POINT

You have a continual moment-to-moment choice where you can follow your habitual thinking, your limiting beliefs, doubts, fears, rules, shoulds and shouldn'ts, or you can follow what you truly want and what you know to be true, your knowing. We have the free will to do either. And neither is inherently wrong. You don't have to follow what you want. It is up to you.

When I ask myself what I want, sometimes the answer is a cup of tea. Sometimes it's a walk. Other times it's a new kitchen. What you want doesn't have to be something big. Wanting is natural; if we follow it, we fill ourselves with excitement, happiness, inspiration, love and presence.

MOMENT BY MOMENT

What if your job were to follow your desire one step at a time?

I used to climb. I wasn't particularly good at it, but I loved it. Once, I was outside, roping up, when I saw a climber next to me at the bottom of a climb. He was looking up at the cliff and moving his arms and legs, mimicking the moves he would make to climb. In my experience, climbers are a friendly bunch, so I asked him what he was doing. "I'm rehearsing the moves I'm going to make," he replied.

When I watched him climb, he was a much more skilled and experienced climber than I was. But what struck me the most is how, as an expert and someone who had clearly climbed the route many a time before, it made sense for him to plan out his moves if he wanted to make the climb as quickly and smoothly as possible.

But for me, I would get to the bottom of the cliff, look where I could place a hand, pull myself up, and then look at where it was obvious to put a foot. From there, I would assess where to place my hand next. One move at a time. I couldn't have possibly planned out my moves because I hadn't done it enough times to have a plan.

The truth is, you don't need to see ten steps ahead, or even three steps ahead. One step at a time is all you need.

'When you walk the way, the way appears.'
(Rumi)

When I first wanted to start up a business, I had a call with a business coach. The first thing they told me to do was to write a business plan. I remember my first thought was "What! I need a plan?"

I had no idea what I was doing. I had no idea what was possible for my business, let alone how to plan to make it happen. I scrapped the planning and just took one step at a time, following what was obvious to me, moment by moment.

Planning doesn't work when you don't already know the climb. It also doesn't work when you want to follow your dreams and you've never done it before.

Sometimes we want things in the moment that might not make immediate sense to us. I recall once thinking that I really needed to write a newsletter to my followers, so I sat down at my desk to write, but really wasn't feeling inspired to write anything. I started to try to come up with something, but it felt forced. This wasn't typical for me as I usually love writing, so I checked in with myself to see what I wanted most in that moment. It turned out that I wanted to take a short break and to walk to the local shop and grab myself a treat.

I remember thinking at the time, "Well, how will that help anyone?" But I knew enough to follow my intuition, and so I went for a short walk and bought my favourite - peanut butter M&Ms. Yum! I took the scenic way home, and enjoyed the sun on my face, the freedom of following my heart, and the sweet taste of the sweets. By the time I was five minutes from home, I was racing back to my desk in order to get my thoughts out of my head and out to my audience!

There might be a reason why you want what you want. Maybe you just need to go for that coffee you want, read that book, or register for that course. The very act of following that inspiration might lead you to your next step.

MAKING DECISIONS

I remember being around sixteen years old and trying to decide whether to go to college or not. I realised I was overthinking it, so I decided to toss a coin: heads, I would go to college, and tails, I would get a full-time job. I was surprised to discover that when the coin landed on heads, I instantly knew that was not what I wanted to do. The coin toss helped me get in touch with my inner wanting and knowing. I remember realising, in fact, that I already knew I wanted to get a full-time job, and was just too caught up in my head to notice.

I started using the coin toss 'technique' to get in touch with my knowing on a regular basis. When I didn't know what to do, I would find that most of the time the coin toss would help me get past my thinking and into a deeper part of me that knew the answer.

What I also found interesting is that sometimes I would toss the coin to get in touch with my knowing, and I would discover that I didn't yet know what I wanted. But I would then *know* that I didn't yet know. At some point, there would come a time when I would know, and until then, I learnt not to overthink it.

No amount of overthinking will help you know something that you don't know.

WANTING NOT NEEDING

Desire feels pleasant. It can feel delightful and meaningful to want something and to be in touch with your wanting, moving forward in a direction that's important to you.

But needing feels very different to wanting. Just like when I thought I needed to earn a certain amount of money to be happy, or have the nice car or a certain qualification. That kind of attachment attributes our happiness outside of ourselves, and that's not where our happiness comes from.

When we attribute our happiness to something outside ourselves, we can get so focused on creating a future, that we lose touch with the feeling of being and presence that we always have available to us right now...

And now...

And now.

There is nothing bad or harmful about desiring something, but we can lose the joy and passion by creating a perpetual state of thinking that we will be happy once we have the required external circumstances.

I once worked with a gymnast who said, "You can be so focused on falling that you lose your focus on balancing." Likewise, in life, we can be so focused on failing or not being able to achieve our dreams that we lose the enjoyment of following what we want. The good news is that it's easy to tell if you're getting attached because you'll know by the feeling you have. If it feels inspiring, pleasurable and light, then you're in touch with your wanting; if it feels stressful, heavy and restrictive, then you're clouded by too much thinking.

So... what is it *you* want?

KEY INSIGHTS

- ◆ You have a wanting. You want what you want, and you have thoughts that get in the way of you pursuing your desires.
- ◆ You have an inner compass of wanting. Following your moment-to-moment inspiration leads to living an inspired life. Following your present happiness creates happiness.
- ◆ You're allowed to have what you want. Wanting is powerful.
- ◆ Anxiety and doubt are nothing more than thoughts. They have no power unless you give them power.
- ◆ You don't need to think too far ahead. Risk assessing/worrying can lead to paralysis. Take one step at a time in the direction of what you want.
- ◆ No amount of overthinking will help you know something that you don't know.
- ◆ Limitation only exists in thought. Possibility is before thought.

FROM INSIGHT TO ACTION

What would you do for the next 5 minutes if you were just following what you wanted without paying attention to any thoughts that might get in the way?

CHAPTER 11

INNER KNOWING

'There is a vast realm of intelligence beyond
thought. Thought is only a tiny aspect of that
intelligence.'
Eckhart Tolle

When I was 15, I was doing some labouring for a builder, using a chop saw to cut bits of material for him to fix onto a roof. He would hand me two different types of material, and my job was to cut each of them to a particular size, depending on the type he gave me.

Each time he passed me a piece, I would ask him how he wanted me to cut it. At one point, he looked at me and said, "Chris, just use your common sense." It might sound daft, but until then, it hadn't occurred to me to do this.

I was surprised to find that when I looked inside, I knew exactly what to do. I had been so concerned about getting it 'right' and looking to someone else for what to do, that I had switched off to what was obvious if only I were to look.

I began to find in life that if I looked beneath my habitual thinking to my common sense, or inner knowing, I would usually know what to do at the time I needed to do it. I also found that if I didn't know what to do, I could just do the next best thing that I knew to do.

I wonder how, if I hadn't been told to use my common sense, when it would have occurred to me to do so. I think so many of us look outside ourselves for answers, whether to other people, or to the rulebook of shoulds, should nots, musts, and must nots, and we forget to look inwards towards our own common sense and wisdom to navigate life.

I like to think of it as we have two ways of navigating life: our personal, habitual thinking and our moment-to-moment inner knowing.

HABITUAL THINKING

Our habitual thinking is the database of things we've already thought. It contains handy information such as where you live, what your favourite food is, what your partner looks like, and perhaps things like how to drive or how to bake a cake.

The fact that our habitual thinking comes from our past is beneficial to know when navigating life and making decisions. If you were to rely solely on the collection of past things you've thought, you could quickly find yourself getting stuck.

I remember when I was once checking into a budget hotel. I walked into the room and was immediately struck by the smell of smoke. I noticed that the smoke alarm had a plastic bag taped over it, so as not to set it off. I took my bags and went to the reception desk to ask for another room. What followed was, to me, quite a comical conversation, as I proceeded to tell the receptionist that the room smelt of smoke and asked to be checked into an alternative room.

"But people aren't allowed to smoke in their rooms." The receptionist answered.

I replied, "Ok, but someone has been smoking in that room. They've even put a plastic bag over the smoke alarm so they didn't set it off."

"But they're not allowed to smoke in their room," was the reply, again.

"But they have. Can I have another room, please?"

"But the rooms have smoke alarms."

The receptionist was so caught up in his head thinking about shoulds and shouldn'ts, that he wasn't paying attention to what was actually happening right in front of him. When he eventually got present, I was able to get another room.

Seeing what's right in front of us is much easier when we're present.

Another way to think about our habitual thinking is your database of thoughts you've already had, or the conditioning you've had up until that point. If you've been programmed to think a certain way about relationships, life, money, religion, politics, or work and use your thinking to navigate these areas of life, you will get more of the same.

I was in London recently and looked up at a building where I saw a large TV screen with the words 'Your expectations are history'.

I have no idea what the advertisement was for, but as I pondered what it meant, I got a deep insight into how we navigate life. Your expectations of life come from your history. In other words, we expect to experience more of what we've already experienced. Furthermore, your expectations shape your experience of the present moment.

I remember when I was out for a run once and I saw what I assumed was a stick on the floor, as I hopped over it, it moved, and I jumped about ten feet in the air when I realised it was a snake! From then on for the next several months, when I was out running, I saw a lot of what I thought were snakes, that were really just sticks. It took quite a while for me, my thinking, and my nervous system to let go of the thought that I would step on a snake, but now it doesn't occur to me anymore.

You can think of this as another example of how confirmation bias shows up in your life, where we tend to direct our awareness to what's familiar and notice things that fit in with what we already know. Our past experiences continue to shape our understanding of life through unconscious predictions, assumptions and expectations.

WAKING UP FROM YOUR HABITUAL FUTURE

Suppose you've had experiences in life where people are untrustworthy. Imagine that you've grown up in a household where your father was particularly untrustworthy and never did the things he said he would do, like show up to football games to watch you play, or attend parents' evenings to talk about your progress at school. In this case, you are highly likely to see these things like untrustworthiness in other people. In other words, you will notice things that fit in with what you've already experienced and see things that confirm that people are untrustworthy.

If you're a physiotherapist and you spend your workdays talking to people about their posture, it's likely that when you're out shopping at the weekend, you can't help but notice other people's posture.

I recall a client explaining to me that because they once had a panic attack in a supermarket, they could no longer go out food shopping and had to order their groceries online. This is an example of being caught up in personal thinking and making a thought-created association where one doesn't inherently exist.

We don't have to navigate life using our conditioning and habitual thinking. But unless we wake up to the present and use our free will, we will have the same experiences without it.

In my experience, we use our free will less than you might think. We are creatures of habit, often drifting through life on autopilot. This is why it's so easy to predict someone's behaviour. Behaviours follow thought, and because we tend to have the same thinking, unless we update it, behaviour becomes predictable.

This is why an alcoholic will stay an alcoholic until they wake up out of the pattern. Or the workaholic will keep working all the hours they can until they burn out. Or people drawn to a particular kind of partner will see the same patterns of argument and conflict arise in their relationships. We live into our habitual future unless we step outside the personal thinking that is causing us to live like we're living.

Unless you're present and in touch with your wisdom, you will be a slave to your programming.

The conditioning you've experienced will run your life in the form of your decisions, actions, and thinking.

Fortunately, you do have free will. Returning to your inner natural wisdom just takes a higher level of awareness. In the same way you can override the autocorrect function on your phone or computer, you can use your free will to override your conditioning. Occasionally, we get caught up in our thinking and do something against our inner knowing, but we can continually return to our inner intelligence and get back on course.

We have an incredible ability to use thought to create things in life. I love using thought to plan an exciting trip, design a new kitchen, or think of all the different things I can build my kids. I really enjoy the process of having something in my mind and then turning into a reality.

But I don't enjoy it when thoughts seem to take me over, and I get lost in worry. This happens when my consciousness is low and my conditioned, habitual thinking has taken over.

'Your Mind is an Excellent Servant, but a Terrible Master.'
(David Foster Wallace)

REAL-TIME NAVIGATION

In addition to our conditioned thinking, we have our own built-in present-moment guidance system, which is available in the form of fresh, new thought or insight.

You might know of it as common sense, intuition, wisdom, instantaneous knowing, or real-time intelligence.

Navigating life using our moment-to-moment inner knowing will produce new experiences, qualitatively different from past experiences. We're made to function using this navigation system, but it's easy to forget that.

I invite you to pause for a moment and ask yourself: Which system do you use the most?

Imagine you have an out-of-date GPS Sat Nav unit. The kind that people used to have in their cars. Now imagine that you're going to be visiting my house, and I'll tell you that I live in a particular village. I also tell you that there is a big hill in that village, the only hill in the village, and that I live in the only house at the top of that hill.

The Sat Nav successfully guides you to the village, where you see the hill. You then see the house, and your common sense says, "That must be Chris's house. He said he lives in the one house on the one hill in this village, and this is the village."

You can even see you're on the road leading up to the house. You're just about to turn the Sat Nav off and follow the obvious route, but then the Sat Nav tells you to turn left to get to your destination.

What do you listen to? Your common sense? Or the Sat Nav?

What amazes me when I ask some of my clients this question is that they sometimes say the Sat Nav.

Whilst it's the most natural thing in the world to follow our common sense and our knowing, unfortunately, many of us get taught not to trust it, and we can even forget it's there altogether. When this happens, instead of naturally following our inspiration and pursuing what we want in life, we do what we think we 'should' do instead.

This results in an unfulfilled life, disconnected from our authentic desires. When this happens, some psychologists refer to it as 'learned hopelessness'. A psychological term used for when we mistakenly think we lack the autonomy and power to have some say over our lives.

Our habitual thinking is like the out-of-date Sat Nav. It's filled with things you learnt from your past, and many of us never take the time to check the validity and relevance of what we actually think.

I like to think of our personal habitual thinking as an accumulation of the training we've had in life.

Imagine that you've started a new job and you're being trained to use a new computer system. You've had your training, and then you're trying to use the system as you've been taught, but it's not working well, and you keep getting stuck. You ask someone next to you what's happening, and they momentarily observe what you're doing. After a minute, they tell you you're not using the system as designed.

"But I read the instruction manual", you say.

"That manual is 30 years out of date", they reply.

In that moment, you would automatically discount what you've learnt and start looking at things afresh, ready to know how it really works.

Many of us have received pretty poor training about how life and psychology actually work. I'm inviting you to consider, now, that if you're getting stuck, you're not using the system as it's designed. Throughout the remainder of this book, I'll be asking you to look towards your own common sense and wisdom rather than your collection of old thoughts to see how things actually work.

It's entirely possible to update our thinking at any given moment. In the present moment, inner knowing is always available if we were only to look towards it. You might have a different name for it. You might call it your intuition, wisdom, instinct, sense, or simply knowing.

If you look inside, you'll find your own words, but these are some of the ways previous clients of mine have identified what I'm pointing towards:

Habitual Thinking	Present Moment Knowing
From the past	Common sense
Out of date	Wisdom
Based on conditioning	Intuitive
'Simply how we've been programmed or what we've thought before'	Gut instinct
	Real-time intelligence
	Instantaneous knowing
Full of shoulds, rules, musts, and other judgments	Obvious at the time
	Natural intelligence
	Wanting/passion
Lacks presence	Explorative
	Spontaneous new thought (creativity)
	Where passion lies
	A feeling of pulling towards something

Here's the truth of what I've learnt, and it is worth restating, over and over…

You can know something without thinking about it.

We all have innate wisdom and the way it shows up is knowing what you need to know, when you need to know it. Wisdom has a feeling to it. So does overthinking. When you know something, it feels obvious and has clarity. It feels clean and clear.

Anxiety, doubt, 'shoulds' and 'shouldn'ts' live in the domain of personal thinking. Possibility, confidence, passion, excitement, joy and aliveness, live in the domain of presence.

One of the easiest times to notice your inner knowing is when you approach a novel situation that isn't like anything you've experienced before. The first time you turn up to school, for example, or the first time you're driving on the motorway. If you know you can't rely on your habitual past thinking to navigate things, you're much more likely to look towards your present moment intelligence to know what to do.

I've known times when people get in touch with their knowing due to the fact that they've hit rock bottom. Think of somebody struggling with alcohol or gambling addiction, losing their house, their loved ones, and their job. While I wouldn't recommend it to anyone, hitting rock bottom can often invite a person to give up on his or her habitual, conditioned thinking and rediscover their inner wisdom instead.

A few days ago, when writing an earlier chapter of this book, my two-year-old daughter wandered into my office to see me. She looked like she needed the toilet, so I said, "Do you need a wee?"

"No", she reflexively replied.

But then I saw her look inwards, and then she said "yes."

It is a simple example, but this clearly demonstrates that our reactive thoughts aren't always the most helpful (or indeed true in the case of my daughter needing the toilet!)

REFLECTION

What do you call your knowing? What's the best word(s) you might use to describe the feeling of it?

Can you think of a time when you followed your inner knowing, despite what habitual thinking you might have had that commanded otherwise?

Do you think you could navigate the next thirty minutes of your life, solely following your inner knowing?

What do you think might get in the way of you following your knowing for the rest of your life?

I tend to find my personal thinking helpful for certain things like booking train tickets and remembering where I live. I don't tend to find it helpful for navigating most day-to-day interactions, or new situations. Because most situations are of course, new, we're always going to want to use our present moment navigation system in order to get the best out of it. We tend to get stuck when we don't use it, and when we've forgotten how reliable it is. Because here's the thing:

Your habitual thinking can't tell you anything new, that you don't already know.

Either you know, or you don't. And no amount of habitual thinking will change that.

What you need is knowing, which comes in the form of new thought, not old habitual thinking. New thoughts come from being open to new thoughts and not from scanning your database of old thinking, and definitely not from overthinking, worry or rumination, which is an internal threat-focused behaviour.

245

Your knowing is what's already and always there, guiding you. That means it is also already there before any habitual thinking you may have. You have an instantaneous knowing that works in real time, that is superior to any habitual thinking. Knowing is before/beneath thinking.

Whilst the information we have stored about some aspects of our past may be invaluable, our wisdom helps discern when to draw on this and when it would be beneficial. Why would you go to an old library when you could look up something online, for example?

In other words, there is an intelligence beyond your habitual thinking that knows when to draw on what you already know, and when to look for fresh new thought.

Many of us are in the habit of looking to what we already think we know, rather than for new thinking. When we don't already know something, it just means that it's not in our filing cabinet of things we've already thought. If we can accept that we don't know, we leave room for insight - a new thought that we haven't thought before. And when we look to insight, we find new ways of being in life that haven't yet occurred to us before. Insight comes from a deeper wisdom beyond our personal thinking.

Neuroscience shows that there is a brain network called the default mode network, which is responsible for creativity and problem-solving. Interestingly, these parts of the brain only come online when you're not focused on an external task. This, in turn, means we can't be truly creative when busy worrying. In other words, when you're ruminating about coming up with an answer to something, overthinking means that your best problem-solving tool (new, creative thought) goes offline.

This is why people often say they have their best ideas in the shower, or when they're out for a walk, not thinking of anything. Occasionally, the best thing you can do when needing an answer to something is to hold a question lightly in your mind and allow yourself to drift in and out of wondering and pondering it. A new idea will come to you when it comes to you, and you will know whether to act on it.

STAGNANT THINKING

Just because we once decided that we don't like lemon cake, we might think this is still true today, even though we haven't tried it for twenty years, and our taste buds have changed.

My wife asked me once if I wanted to go out for dinner at the weekend. I said I'd love to, and she started giving me options for where we might go. At one point, she said the name of a restaurant and then quickly followed that up with "Oh, we can't go there because you don't like it."

"What makes you say that?" I asked.

"Because you said you went there once, and it was awful."

"When did I say that?" I asked.

"A few years ago." She replied.

She was right, I did say that. But I burst out laughing, as I realised I hadn't been to the restaurant in over twenty years!

"Let's go," I said. And we had a great meal.

Just because you used to think something, doesn't mean you would think it now.

Another client of mine once came to me because they were struggling with anxiety about an upcoming presentation at work.

Steven: I'm just not very articulate.

Chris: Hmm, that's strange, you say that. I've not experienced that with you at all.

Steven: Well, you're just being nice.

Chris: No, not at all. Not once have you seemed to struggle to convey what you wanted to me, and not once have I not understood you. When did you decide you're not articulate?

Steven: Oh. Well, I used to think that when I was a kid and we had to read in class.

Chris: What happened?

Steven: All the other kids seemed to read really well, and I stumbled over my words.

Chris: When was this?

Steven: When I was about 11.

Chris: And how old are you now?

Steven: 53.

Chris: Huh. So, 42 years ago, you decided you weren't very articulate. Do you think you've got any better since then at articulating yourself?

Steven: Ha ha, yeah, I didn't realise I was still believing that. Everyone always tells me how good a communicator I am.

Chris: So what's the problem again?

Steven: I can't see one now!

The problem was not in the presentation my client had to give; the problem was that they were living in a thought-created reality where they couldn't articulate themselves. Being nervous makes perfect sense inside this stagnant thinking, but when you see things as novel, and use your moment-to-moment intuition and awareness, you're free from any feeling the stagnant thinking was creating.

My client simply hadn't updated his thinking, like he was using an old computer programme, or an out-of-date map, to navigate the situation.

FORGETTING OUR COMMON SENSE

Although we can get conditioned out of trusting our common sense and can become habitually switched off to our inner knowing, the moment we look for it, it's still always there.

Most of the time, when one of my clients gets a significant insight, they just go 'oh yeah', as they recognise that what I'm saying makes perfect sense and they already knew it.

From my experience, I've often found that when we're stuck in life, it's because we're not acting using our intelligence, and it's likely we've defaulted into following our limited habitual thinking.

We're designed so that we don't need to carry our baggage around with us. We can just rely on our present-moment knowing to guide us.

A friend of mine was talking to me the other day about their newborn baby and the struggles they were having keeping to their schedule. When I asked what schedule, they told me they were following a timetable of when to wake their baby up, when to breastfeed, when to put them down for a nap, and when to play with them, all down to the minute.

My friend had been having a tricky time, so they relied on what had worked for someone else and followed that, hoping it would work for them. Even though it wasn't working for them, they felt so helpless that they forgot to look in the one place where they always find the answers. Their inner wisdom. They were so focused on what they should be doing that they dismissed their better knowing and intuition.

When I next saw my friend, they had thrown the schedule out, and things were working wonderfully because they were making it up as they went along, but tuned into their intuition and the baby's needs.

We each listen to our natural intelligence to a greater or lesser degree. We can go years without tapping into it and instead, follow our habitual, conditioned thinking.

FOLLOWING YOUR KNOWING

So many people tell me that they don't know what they want. But it's only because they haven't looked. Usually, either their personal thinking is too loud, or they don't think that they are allowed to have what they want.

We all have our passions and interests. There's always something or someone that inspires us. What if we are here to follow that excitement or inspiration?

If you want more happiness in your life, it's simple: follow your happiness. If you want a happy life, you create that in the moment (and in the future) by filling your moments with the things that make you happy. The only obstacle to that is your habitual thinking.

I find that the more my clients get to know and trust this state of being, of knowing, the more they sink into a natural kind of flow state, and the higher performance and wellbeing they tend to experience.

KEY INSIGHTS

- ◆ We can either live in thought or we can live in presence. And what is always present is your knowing and your wanting.
- ◆ We can look for fresh new thoughts every moment, rather than relying on our out-of-date, conditioned thinking.
- ◆ If you don't update your thinking, you get stuck having more of the same.

◆ Relying on habitual, conditioned thinking leaves you drifting through life, rather than open to presence and possibility.

◆ It's much easier to make decisions when you're present without carrying the baggage of your old thinking around with you.

FROM INSIGHT TO ACTION

If you didn't take your thinking so seriously, what might that change for you?

CHAPTER 12

PERFORMANCE

'The more you do, the more you can do.'
Steve Chandler

There's a certain kind of high performance that's natural. Natural means that it's not forced, not pressured, not hard work, and not stressful. In fact, it's organic and effortless. If you've ever heard of someone talking about being in alignment, flow, the zone, or synchronicity, the chances are that they are all pointing towards the same kind of natural performance.

This natural performance comes when we're in action, without too much thinking. What's more, we all know this experience.

FLOW STATE

In the work on flow state by Mihaly Csikszentmihalyi, he states that flow state is achieved when certain conditions are met:

- You are focused on the task at hand
- You have clear goals
- There is feedback between our action and the goal
- There is a loss of self-consciousness
- There is a sense of control and an absence of worry
- There is an optimal balance between your level of skill and the activity

In other words, when we're not thinking about ourselves or worrying about doing it right, we have a clear mind and find ourselves in a state of flow.

It's a beautiful state of presence where we lose awareness of ourselves and our awareness merges with the activity in front of us.

Flow is linked to happiness and enjoyment, so we can also find ourselves in this harmonious experience when we don't have too much on our minds. We have more consciousness, less thought.

'One acts with a deep but effortless involvement that removes from awareness the worries and frustrations of everyday life.'
(Mihaly Csikszentmihalyi)

With flow state comes enjoyment and a sense of freedom.

One of the things I've come to see is that rather than flow state being something to manufacture, it is actually my natural state. I don't need to think about something in order to create flow state; I simply drop into it when I get beneath my thinking.

Here are some characteristics of flow state that my clients have articulated over the years;

ENJOYMENT
LIGHT
LOST IN TIME
ENERGISED
THE ZONE
FLOWING
FREEDOM
LOVE
JOY
ALIVENESS
NATURAL

This state is in contrast to one of forced effort and action, which can be characterised by;

Stress
Boredom
Overthinking
Effort
Fire fighting
Things looking hard or impossible

Worry or anxiety
Heaviness
Burdensome
Feeling lost or lacking in clarity

I remember the first time I saw the contrast between these two states. I was 15 and was working in my local pub, washing up. One busy weekend, in the evening, I noticed how two chefs with equal responsibilities had two entirely different experiences whilst cooking.

One of the chefs, Vicky, was clearly stressed, flustered, and overwhelmed with her thinking about the number of food orders they had to cook. The other chef, Richard, was in a clear state of flow. He was enjoying himself, was light-hearted, and enthusiastic as he cooked and prepared the food.

What struck me even more than their contrasting internal experience was how they also performed differently in their actions.

Vicky was visibly panicking, would sometimes drop food on the floor, and would often be short-tempered with the waiting staff. She would get caught up in her head from time to time, which slowed her down and made her less productive. Richard, on the other hand, was in flow state, productive, helpful to the waiting staff, and organised.

Richard made it look effortless, so much that it might be misinterpreted that he didn't care, but he was in the optimum condition for both performance and enjoyment.

This was the first time I remember being consciously aware of the power of thought-created experience in a real-life situation. It became obvious to me that it wasn't the situation that caused the stress, but the inner psychology of the people involved.

So, how do we go from being like Vicky to being like Richard and getting the most out of life?

In short, the less thinking we have, the more we create what we want, leading to more inspiration. The more action we tend to take, the more results we tend to get. It looks like this:

INSPIRATION
EXCITMENT
WANTING

RESULTS

ACTION

I like to think of performance as what happens when you take action and don't let your thinking get in the way.

NATURAL PERFORMANCE AND FLOW

Remember that flow state is normal. If we look at Richard, we might compare his state to that of a young child, who will frequently get immersed in what they're doing, fully engaged in their activity.

If a child is able to do this without any training in how to get into flow state, we all can, because it is inherent and natural.

If I had to guess, I'd say Vicky was thinking something like "I can't handle this, it's too much". It looks like this;

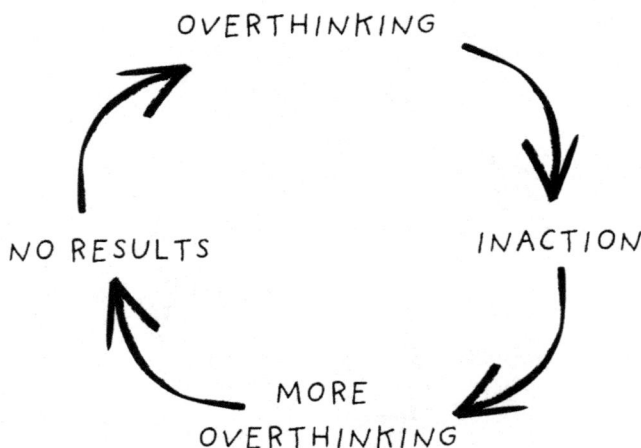

OVERTHINKING

NO RESULTS

INACTION

MORE
OVERTHINKING

The only difference between Vicky and Richard was that he wasn't thinking that it was too much to handle.

Remember that for flow state, we need an absence of self-consciousness, and no thinking about the end result or worrying if we can achieve it. When you take away this worry, you drop into presence and action.

Earlier in the book, I mentioned that you don't need to think your way out of a thought-created problem. Whilst this is true, you also can't think your way out of a real problem. For a real problem, you need action. And with less thinking, we tend to have more action.

When you think of any toddler beginning to take their first steps, consider how many fall over when learning to walk. No doubt all of them. They just don't have any thinking about it. They don't make falling mean anything. They want to walk so that they can get places. So they walk, they fall, they get back up again, and they repeat, until they learn the skill.

If you compare that to some adults who want to learn a skill, we fail, we make it mean that we're a failure, and we often give up.

When I've occasionally worked with high-performing athletes, they seem to all have the same thing in common. They deal with mistakes and failure like children. They don't make it mean anything. So what if high performance comes naturally to us when we don't get in the way with our thinking?

"I couldn't do what I do if I took my personal thinking so seriously."
(*Said anyone who is a high performer)

Now I'm not suggesting for a minute that we could all become high-performing athletes. But would we all want to? The Olympics would get pretty busy, with everyone on the track and no one in the audience to spectate!

What I am suggesting is that we all have our own things we want to pursue. And if we followed our desires, and not our limited thinking, we'd have more of what we want, and less of what we don't want.

When you know that your feelings aren't bound or tied to circumstances, you're more free to play around with ideas and create cool things in the world. Because you're not basing your wellbeing on external situations, you have more room for creativity, action taking, and better results.

Because we experience life and circumstance via thought, it becomes a game of mastering our inner world, not the outer. When you master the inner world, creating results in the outside world becomes far easier.

Life is a constant flow; when we're not flowing, it's because we're trying to go against how it flows.

GOING AGAINST THE FLOW

There's a fundamental difference between thinking that flow state is somewhere to get to, and realising that it's something to drop or sink into. I was exploring this with a client when they told me they couldn't possibly get into flow state because they had too much to do.

They used the metaphor of laying train tracks and needing to be finished before they could relax. Before I could answer, my client said, "Oh, I guess I can be in flow state whilst I'm laying the tracks!"

They saw for themselves, there and then, that stress was a

choice, and that overthinking tends to lead to underperformance and often inaction.

Another client I worked with, called James, was under the impression that overthinking was actually helpful to them. Here's the moment when they started to see things differently:

Chris: I tend to find that overthinking leads to stress, and stress isn't really very helpful for getting things done.

James: No, stress helps me get things done.

Chris: How? Why would you need stress to act intelligently and productively?

James: Well, I put some of my success down to stress.

Chris: I would say that 100% of your success comes down to your intelligence, and none of it to stress. You lose intelligence when you're stressed. The creative problem-solving parts of your brain go offline with stress because it's a threat focused state of survival. So, rather than having access to your intelligence and common sense, stressful thoughts are the only things you'll be thinking when you're stressed. It's effectively like your brain is shrinking. Why would that help you get things done?

James: That's true. When I come out of the stress, I always look back and see that it was a waste of time and energy.

Chris: Exactly. And it often takes coming out of the stress to realise that. What if it could become a genuine choice never to stay stressed? I'm not saying you won't, but you can come out of it when you see you're in it, and that it's

261

not helpful. You'll find that you have moments of stress, but they won't last. Lots of little experiences of stress throughout the day, perhaps, but they will pass quicker and quicker the more you see that it's never helpful.

James: Yes, then I'd be more successful, not less. I see that now.

When people see that stress is optional and unhelpful, they actually experience it less.

I remember noticing a fundamental shift in my understanding of stress when I once sat down and consciously tried to rest my mind.

Usually, I would start revving my mind up when I was stressed to try to solve the problem outside of myself. But instead, this time I found myself knowing I needed to slow my thinking down.

Because we are living in the feeling our thinking, not the feeling of our circumstance, when we're feeling stressed, we need less thinking not more.

I knew it was nothing outside of my thinking that was causing me stress. And I knew the answer was to have less thinking and more clarity.

GETTING OUT OF OUR OWN WAY

Suppose you want to create something in your life: financial success, a thriving business, an intimate relationship, or a happy family. In that case, I'd invite you to ponder for a moment that all those things could either be created from force and effort, or from a place of joy and effortlessness.

It's helpful to know that when we're stressed and anxious, our IQ actually drops. There's more intelligence in feelings of happiness and clarity than there is in feelings of anxiety.

What's more, following your anxious feelings won't lead you anywhere happy.

Here's a reminder from chapter one:

'Most of us, most of the time, are using our minds innocently and unconsciously, creating things we don't really want to create. But when we learn more about how our mind works, we can begin to create more of what we want, and less of what we don't want, releasing more potential and higher performance.'

If you want to be happy, anxious thinking is the wrong tool for the job. It's like trying to fit a square in a round hole, or trying to hammer in a nail with a screwdriver. It simply doesn't work.

So why trust your anxious thinking more than your inner wisdom and happiness?

Here's the thing I've learnt over my lifetime of studying human performance that I believe explains why we don't all naturally perform well all the time;

If you're saying that you want to do something but you aren't doing it, then it's because it doesn't fully make sense to you to do it.

In other words, if you're not already pursuing what you say you want, it's because you're unconsciously assuming that you will lose something by having it or by pursuing it.

I remember when I first glimpsed this phenomenon in my old psychotherapy practice. I was with a client who was struggling with health anxiety. She was often in and out of GP surgeries due to various worries about her health. She would spend hours researching multiple symptoms and seeking reassurance from her mother and boyfriend about various lumps and bumps on her body, which never amounted to anything.

We had worked together for a couple of months, and I'd tried everything I knew to help her with her anxious thoughts, feelings and habits. She was bright, and I was baffled as to why nothing seemed to work, with no change whatsoever.

One session, when I'd pretty much run out of ideas to help her, I wondered out loud to her, "Can you think of any reasons why you might not want to get rid of this anxiety?"

I hadn't actually expected an answer, but to my surprise, she paused for a moment to genuinely ponder the question.

After a while, she looked at me, shocked and upset and said "oh".

"What?" I asked

"If I got rid of this anxiety, I wouldn't get any attention."

She was genuinely surprised to have discovered this for herself. It was an unconscious intention that she had created at some point in her life to receive attention from people around her.

What I then realised was this:

It made perfect sense to her to experience her worries about her health.

Even though it was unconscious, she didn't want to get rid of the problem she was coming to see me for, because it could create a new problem for her. (The lack of attention.)

Imagine that you have a problem. Something you say you don't like or want in your life. You've been trying to solve this problem for years, but nothing you try seems to work.

What if on some level it doesn't make sense to you to solve that problem?

RESISTANCE TO CHANGE

Whenever there's resistance to change, or when someone wants to change but doesn't seem to be able to, it's often because the change they are imagining, is worse than their current reality.

What if somewhere outside your current awareness, there is a thought keeping your problems and struggles alive?

Let's meet Beth, a client I worked with who came to see me because she was in what she called a 'lifeless marriage'. She was no longer in love with her husband and she wanted to separate. She worked part-time doing a job she loved, and she adored her two children. She described how it felt as if she was trapped in a prison and wanted to get out, but simply couldn't see an exit.

Beth was often inconsistent in how she talked about the relationship and would sometimes describe how much she wanted to leave, and at other times would say that it wasn't that bad.

When I pointed out the ambivalence to her, she asked me if I thought she was in denial.

Chris: I don't know, but I'm just checking in with you to see what you really want.

Beth: I just don't see what's possible for me outside the marriage.

Chris: I didn't ask what you think is possible. I asked what you want.

Beth: Oh. Well, I don't want him to move out. He'll take the kids with him, and I'll be left lost, lonely and with no money.

Chris: No wonder you're feeling stuck with this if that's the future you're imagining. That sounds like moving from one prison to another.

Beth: Oh yeah.

Chris: If that's the only possibility you're imagining for yourself, why would you take steps to make that happen? It wouldn't make any sense.

Beth: Good point. It's like I've been decorating my current prison instead of taking the steps to escape.

Chris: Yes, you have a future of pure possibility, and you've been painting a picture of limitation. And a very scary one at that! Can you now see how this fabricated image is keeping you stuck in your current situation?

Beth: Yes, absolutely!

Chris: Perhaps you could create a new image for your future self?

Beth: Oh yes, I like that!

When people feel stuck, it's usually because the thing they're thinking of changing doesn't really make sense to them to change. This can often be unconscious until they make it conscious.

In the movie, The Shawshank Redemption, there is a man in prison who's been incarcerated for so long that he can't imagine what it would be like once he's released. In fact, just before he's up for parole, he attacks another inmate to ensure he's not released. It's a great example of how familiarity can feel safe and known, even if it's not an ideal situation.

REFLECTION

Consider a problem or pattern in your life that you often find yourself wondering about or talking about with others. Would you have any imagined concerns if we could remove that struggle for you?

Be genuinely curious to see what comes to mind and complete the following sentence;

I don't want to get rid of this problem because...

What resistance do you have towards creating what you say you want to create?

THINKING PRECEDES ACTION

If performance comes from action, and action comes from what we're thinking, then we need to look towards our thinking when it comes to getting results. And here's the thing;

Everything we do makes perfect sense to us based on our conscious or unconscious thinking.

If I believed the Earth was flat, I would be highly cautious whenever I went out sailing, and I'd think anybody flying around the world must be insane.

If you want to change something, you must first change how it makes sense to you. If you invite someone who thinks the Earth is flat to sail around the world with you, you must first change their thinking.

If you want to drop an unhelpful behaviour or habit, then you're going to have to look to see why the habit makes sense to you first, before you drop it. Otherwise, any change will feel forced, and you'll rely on pure willpower to power through any change. When you change how things make sense to you, you won't need any willpower because things will look different to you.

We do what makes sense to us, and we don't do what doesn't make sense to us.

CONFLICTING INTENTIONS

I remember when I was five months into my coaching business, struggling to make enough money, I took the problem to my coach at the time, and he wondered if I was using my time productively to grow my business, seeing as that's what I said I wanted.

He asked me to tell him how I spent my workday. I told him that after waking up, I'd usually spend some time with my newborn son, and then I'd do a couple of emails. After that, I would head to the gym, do a workout, have lunch there and do a couple more emails and maybe a client session.

I was embarrassed and genuinely surprised when my coach laughed at me. But at that moment, I saw what he saw.

No wonder I was struggling. I was working about 2 hours a day! I'd fallen into a perpetual self-employed kind of holiday, which was a huge blind spot for me.

When he then asked me what I thought was keeping me from a full workday and ultimately success, I realised that I had an image in my mind of me being incredibly busy with work, oversubscribed, burnt out and never having any free time, and ending up unfulfilled in life.

It was an unconscious image I had in my mind, keeping me from growing my business. I honestly couldn't see it until that point, and once I saw the mind-made conflict for what it was, my business accelerated to me running a successful full coaching practice within two months.

When someone's stuck, it's because they're consciously or unconsciously imagining a future that's worse than the one they're currently stuck in.

Our thoughts about an imagined future create our experience right now in the present moment and drive our actions.

Sometimes the key is seeing that your imaginary future is not your actual future.

It's like we say we want something, but we also have a conflicting unconscious idea that we don't want it. A concern about what would happen if we let go of the problem we say we don't want.

When we can make the concern or conflicting intention conscious enough, it no longer looks valid. We're able to let it go and move in a direction that feels important to us.

Things are easy to drop when you don't want them and don't make sense to you.

I recall a session where someone very quickly saw for themselves that their unconscious idea of an imagined future kept them stuck.

The client, Craig, came to me because he'd been struggling with anxiety for decades and had reportedly tried everything to find more peace and ease in life, but nothing had worked.

Craig was very resistant to anything I had to say, but at the same time, he didn't want to give up when I suggested that he might be better off with another coach. In one session, when we explored what it might be like for him to find inner peace, he suddenly looked more tense than ever.

Chris: What just went through your mind?

Craig: If I find inner peace, then I'll lose my personality and won't be able to function.

Chris: That's very different to how I understand inner peace.

Craig: How do you understand it?

Chris: As peaceful. A feeling of contentment, joy, and clarity. A sense of ease and flow. You didn't describe peace. You described more anxious thinking.

Craig: Oh yeah. But I'm scared that if I get more peaceful, I'll lose myself.

Chris: Well, you're currently imagining a future whilst looking through the lens of anxiety. When you're actually peaceful, you won't have that anxious thinking.

Craig: That makes sense. So what do I need to do?

Chris: I don't think you need to do anything. If you let that scary thought of your imagined future go, you'll naturally find yourself at peace.

Craig went away and processed the truth of this and found himself much more peaceful and able to easily dismiss anxious thoughts when he saw their true, illusory nature.

STUCK IN THOUGHT

A client came to me wanting my help pursuing a particular project they were passionate about. They explained how much they wanted to engage in the work and how excited they were to begin, but they were getting stuck. The project would take about two years, and they were concerned about then having to market it, as marketing was something they deeply disliked doing.

I replied, "So let me see if I heard this right. You can't wait to get started, you've secured funding for two years, and you're good to go. But you're thinking of an imagined obstacle two years from now, and that's what's getting you stuck?"

I had been working with this client for a while, and they instantly saw what they were doing to themselves. They were creating an obstacle to start the project right now, when in reality, there was no real problem at all.

My client chuckled as their level of consciousness rose to one where their previous thinking looked laughable to them.

Any future imagined problem you have today about following your passions, desires, and dreams is just a thought. We live in a world of pure possibility, but we look through the lens of limitation, anxiety and doubt. It's not uncommon for participants to say after one of my workshops that they can do anything they want to do, or be anyone they want to be. They've stepped outside their habitual thinking into the space where anything is possible.

MOVING FORWARD

The more we overthink something or think about our thinking, the more lost we get inside our heads, and the less we're in action. We don't need more stress and anxiety. We need more natural intelligence and inspiration.

The more you follow the feelings of inspiration, passion and excitement, without too much thinking about how to get there, or the end result, the more this leads to inspired action and inevitable results.

Fortunately for all of us, it's easy to know which one you're relying on to navigate life, since overthinking has a feeling to it, and so does clarity and inspiration.

KEY INSIGHTS

◆ We can achieve our natural flow state when we focus on a task with a clear goal, and we don't think about ourselves or worry whether we are doing it right.

◆ Performance is what happens when you take action and don't let your thinking get in the way of that action.

◆ Things flow when you work with them and stop fighting them or denying them.

◆ Flow state is natural and always there beneath the surface of your thinking. You drop into flow state rather than create it.

◆ Stress is unhelpful, as it shuts off the creative problem-solving parts of your brain and lowers your intelligence. It is also optional. When you see this you will experience stress less.

◆ We can create anything in life and do anything from a place of presence and flow, or we can create from a place of stress or anxiety - it's our choice.

◆ If you are struggling to solve a problem, it may be you are resisting the change because it doesn't fully make sense for you to solve that problem, and the change you are imagining is worse than your current reality.

FROM INSIGHT TO ACTION

Bring a project or activity to mind that you know you do really well in. It might be something like cooking, painting, or marketing. Now bring something to mind that doesn't seem to flow so easily. What might it be like to bring the same sense of presence and flow as you do with the first activity to the second?

CHAPTER 13

FINAL THOUGHTS

'One insight is all you need to change your life forever'.
Chris Finn

Sometimes in my work, I witness some incredible transformations in a very short space of time. What follows is a real story of a life-changing insight that happened in a single moment from someone who suffered from years of trauma and abuse.

Rita came to see me following a recommendation from a friend of hers that I'd worked with. Rita told me that she'd tried everything, but nothing had helped her overcome years of depression, anxiety and post-traumatic stress disorder (PTSD).

When Rita asked me if I thought I could help, I was honest with her and told her I didn't know, but that I do find my approach is quite different from anything else.

One of the things I found with Rita was that despite having had a traumatic past, she instantly trusted me, and I think that was the reason we were able to bring about such positive change so quickly.

Rita asked me if she should start off our first session together by explaining to me about her past and all the bad things that had happened to her.

Chris: No, please don't do that. I think that would probably bring both of us down!

Rita: Oh. Well, how will you help me if you don't know about all the terrible things that have happened to me?

Chris: I don't know yet, but I do know that it won't help to keep thinking about all these terrible things. I'm guessing you've already tried talking about it all and that it hasn't helped?

Rita: Yes, lots of times. I've had counselling, CBT, DBT, EMDR, and just about everything else. Nothing has helped, and I don't like talking about all the past stuff.

Chris: Can I ask, if you don't like talking about it, why do you?

Rita: Because I thought I needed to. Doesn't it help process it?

Chris: I'm not sure it does. I think maybe it just keeps you thinking about it, and when you think about those hurtful things, you feel the hurt as if it were happening again right now?

Rita: Yes, that's what happens. But sometimes I think about it, and I don't want to. And I feel as if I'm back there.

Chris: Yes, that sounds like what we might call trauma. Without going into the details, when you think about what happened, what's the worst bit?

Rita: How my Father ruined my life.

Chris: I'm sorry to hear that. How long ago did all this happen?

Rita: About forty years.

Chris: And does what he did then still ruin your life now?

Rita: Yes. I'd like to forgive him, but I don't see how I can.

Chris: Do you still see him now?

Rita: Yes.

Chris: And does he still continue to hurt you?

Rita: No, and I'd love to have a better relationship with him, but I just can't forgive him for what he's done.

Chris: I'm just wondering, what exactly is it that you want to forgive him for?

Rita: For making me feel that I'm broken.

Chris: Ah, ok. And how often do you think that?

Rita: All the time. All day. Every day.

Chris: That sounds like a lot to forgive him for.

Rita: Yes, it is.

Chris: So, what if you didn't need to forgive him for that bit?

Rita: What do you mean?

Chris: Well, your Dad did what he did to you, but I'm wondering where the story that you're broken came from?

Rita: From him.

Chris: Well, yes, I know it must look that way to you. But whatever he did, that story was made up in your head. So maybe you don't need to forgive your Dad for that part? And please remember that I'm appealing to your inner knowing here and not your habitual thinking.

(At this point of the conversation, I was nervous to point this out to Rita, but I trusted in our relationship, and my intuition told me that Rita very much wanted to be free from the pain).

Rita: Hang on. So you're saying that I made that bit up?

Chris: Didn't you? I'm not saying it wasn't completely understandable. But whatever your Dad did was because of him, and him alone. It didn't and doesn't say anything about you. You made up a story that what he did meant you were broken. And that happened in your mind.

Rita: Oh.

Chris: What's going on for you?

Rita: I don't need to forgive him for ruining my life. I just need to forgive him for what he actually did.

Chris: Yes.

Rita: But what he did was wrong.

Chris: Yes, I have no doubt of that.

Rita: And that's what I need to forgive him for. Not for me thinking I was broken.

Chris: That's right. And how often do you tell yourself that you're broken?

Rita: Oh my god. It's me. I'm creating it! I'm the one who continually tells myself that. For forty years!

Chris: Yes, but innocently. So you can forgive yourself for that, too.

Rita: Yes. (looking calm and relieved).

Chris: How's that for you now?

Rita: Everything feels different. I remember once someone saying how your past doesn't define you. But now I see that for myself. I don't have to carry this baggage around anymore. He did what he did, but I don't need to keep telling myself the story.

Chris: You look free.

Rita: I am.

In a very short space of time, Rita saw that something had happened, and she was carrying around a narrative of that experience for many years. I kept in touch with Rita, and she's doing great and living a happy life. All because she saw the separation between what happened outside herself and what happened in her own mind. When Rita was able to drop her thinking, she fell into her wellbeing and true nature.

FINAL WORDS

As we are now at this final chapter, let's take a moment to reflect on what we've been exploring together throughout these pages.

I've shared some simple yet life-changing insights about how our experience is fundamentally shaped by thought. My hope is that you've seen for yourself just how much your own personal experience of life is created from the inside-out and how we shape each moment of our life.

For me, what once seemed like unchangeable outside circumstances, I now recognise as illusions of limitation created by my mind. I hope you've glimpsed the ever-present freedom and possibility that is your birthright, waiting for you to notice.

These understandings are liberating: no matter what is happening around you, you hold the keys to your own experience. If a long-held trauma can dissolve for someone in one illuminating moment, freedom can happen for you, too. As we bring this book to a close, I'll leave you with a reminder from chapter two...

Babies are born inherently free. For them, life is pure potential, opportunity, and possibility.

If we're born inherently free, with pure possibility in front of us, why don't we feel this way? What changed?

I'm going to tell you the answer...

Nothing.

Nothing changed.

At times, you're going to forget that. But that's ok. As soon as you remember, you're free again.

Take a moment to consider your own life. What dreams or changes have been whispering to you from inside? Maybe there's a career you yearn to explore, a relationship you want to heal, or an adventure you've imagined. Perhaps you've already felt a quiet nudge of inspiration or noticed a fresh perspective on something that once seemed impossible. What if the only thing between you and that life is an old thought you no longer need to believe?

My parting invitation is this: trust the wisdom within you. The insights we've explored aren't just ideas on a page— they're meant to be lived. I wonder what might happen if you take the key insights from the end of each chapter and actually live them?

By "live them", I mean live as if they were true.

It's so easy to get caught up in what we might call life. But it's not really life, is it? We get caught up in our minds and in the day-to-day grind of making a living and getting through the busy routines.

What might your life look like if you followed your heart and wisdom? What might the world look like if everyone were in touch with their heart, their innate wisdom and dropped any thoughts that hurt them or hurt others? What then?

ACKNOWLEDGEMENTS

Without you, the reader I never would have been able to create this book, and there certainly wouldn't be anyone to read it. Thank you for your interest in this work of freedom. I hope you've gained as much from the insights I've shared as I have.

To my wife, Emma, who has been invaluable in the creation of this book. Not only is she an incredible wife and Mother, but she's also an excellent proof-reader, and the one who reminds me to read my own book when I'm caught up in my own limiting stories and can't see clearly! Without Emma, this book would not exist.

To my editor, Sean, thank you for believing in me and for helping me turn this work from something on my computer screen, into something real that will make a positive difference in the world.

To my bro, Jon Prince, thank you for continually inspiring me and inviting me up to be the highest version of myself.

To Michael Neill, my mentor who taught me so much about finding my own happiness. Thank you for teaching me the inside-out understanding, and for training me to help others find their own joy in life.

To Richard Goldie, my first coach. Thank you for asking me what I wanted, and for setting me on my path. I will never forget you. R.I.P.

What started off with a few phone notes and emails to myself from my twenty years of study, has resulted in this book – *A Clear Mind*. My only hope is that this book has left you with just that. I believe that when we have a clear mind, we feel connected to our true self, and we follow our hearts desire. And I think that's what we all long for.

ABOUT THE AUTHOR

Chris Finn is a transformative life coach based in Dorset, with twenty years of experience working in psychology. Chris has worked as a Senior Psychotherapist, Mindfulness Teacher, a Wellbeing Lead in the NHS, and Senior Lecturer at University.

Specialising in wellbeing and performance coaching, Chris employs a unique approach that focuses on a less is more mindset. Chris works with individuals, groups and businesses to help people remove limiting beliefs to uncover wellbeing, resilience and high performance.

You can find Chris at www.chris-finn.com or by scanning the QR code below:

Printed in Dunstable, United Kingdom